Early American Wars and Military Institutions

Dave Richard Palmer
James W. Stryker

Thomas E. Griess
Series Editor

DEPARTMENT OF HISTORY
UNITED STATES MILITARY ACADEMY
WEST POINT, NEW YORK

AVERY PUBLISHING GROUP INC.
Wayne, New Jersey

Illustration Credits

The authors and editor gratefully acknowledge the use of a series of paintings commissioned by the U.S. Army Center of Military History. Painted by H. Charles McBarron, these illustrations were presented in *Soldiers of the American Revolution*.

The publisher would like to thank Dr. George Lankevich for the use of his historical library collection.

Series Editor, Thomas E. Griess
In-House Editor, Joanne Abrams.
Cover design by Martin Hochberg.

Library of Congress Cataloging-in-Publication Data

Palmer, Dave Richard, 1934-
   Early American wars and military institutions.

   (The West Point military history series)
   Bibliography: p.
   Includes index.
   1. United States--History, Military--To 1900.
2. Military art and science--United States--History--18th century. 3. Military art and science--United States--History--19th century. 4. United States--History--Revolution, 1775-1783--Campaign. 5. United States--History--War of 1812--Campaigns. 6. United States--History--War with Mexico, 1845-1848--Campaigns.
I. Title. II. Series.
E181.P5   1986   973   86-17281

ISBN 0-89529-324-2
ISBN 0-89529-264-5 (pbk.)

10 9 8 7 6 5 4 3 2 1

Printed in the United States of America

Contents

To Professor Theodore Ropp, whose skill
in sparking intellectual curiosity is reflected in this work.

Illustrations

Maps

Foreword

For almost a century, cadets at the United States Military Academy have studied military campaigns and institutions in a classroom setting. Only in recent years, however, has the course entitled History of the Military Art included coverage of the early American experience in military affairs. In 1973, the Department of History began using an interim, departmentally-prepared text that recounted how the early Americans waged war and examined the considerations that influenced the military policy which the United States adopted in the early years of its existence.

Early American Wars and Military Institutions was conceived as a text that would introduce the student to the American military system in its earliest form. The decision to begin the narrative with the American Revolutionary War was an arbitrary one, made in the full realization that an argument can be advanced for including the colonial wars in such an account as this. While this argument attracts support in some quarters, it is nevertheless true that until Americans had full and sole responsibility for their national defense, the cornerstones of military policy were not established.

National military institutions are influenced by a combination of social, political, economic, geographical, and military factors. In the case of the United States, one can add to these a cultural ingredient that had its roots in a European heritage. All of these factors are considered in this text. Because they are so dominant in the structuring of the narrative, however, a central theme that appears in other texts in The West Point Military History Series—the evolution of the art of war—receives considerably less emphasis in this text. Nevertheless, treated in their unique early American setting, several factors that are important to an evolving art of war are examined in the narrative. Strategy, generalship, civil-military relations, and professionalism are

four of these factors.

Two faculty members of the Department of History at the United States Military Academy shared in the writing of this text. Because of limited classroom time, they dealt only with the bare essentials of the story. Relying largely upon sound secondary sources, they produced a narrative that combines operational and institutional treatments of military history, thus offering a broader scope for teaching application. The Department of History as well as many students are indebted to them for their efforts, which were made under the pressure of time and with minimal resources. Dave R. Palmer wrote the first two chapters, which recount the fighting of the Revolutionary War. A key theme in Palmer's account is the changing strategy employed by George Washington. James W. Stryker prepared the final two chapters, which are devoted largely to institutional military history. He traces the development of United States military policy in the 50 years following the Revolution.

The present edition of *Early American Wars and Military Institutions* is essentially the text that was published at the Military Academy in 1979. As editor, I have added an introductory section, attempted to clarify certain passages for the general reader, amplified purely military terminology, and tried to improve the evenness of the narrative. I gratefully acknowledge the assistance of Dave R. Palmer in providing additional material regarding Washington's strategy. The editor is grateful also for the advice and suggestions that were tendered by Rudy Shur and Joanne Abrams of Avery Publishing Group, Inc. Their assistance was timely and helpful. Ms. Abrams immeasurably improved the narrative through her painstaking editing, corrections of lapses in syntax, and penetrating questions related to clarity of expression.

Thomas E. Griess
Series Editor

Introduction

In a large sense, the American Revolutionary War was but one phase of the long-standing confrontation between France and England. Backwash from the colonial wars spawned the rebellion; and French support, both moral and physical, helped keep the Americans fighting. Ultimately, it became a world war between England and continental powers, with North America being, in a sense, one theater of that war. After it was all over, and the colonies had secured their independence, antagonism between Paris and London continued, leading eventually to a day of final reckoning at Waterloo. Saying that the American Revolution was part of the Anglo-French conflict, however, can be misleading. The War of Independence was affected mightily by European events, to be sure, but it was also a self-contained, homegrown affair, at once depending on and independent of European pressures. It was a war within a war.

From the stand at Lexington to the siege at Yorktown, the very vocabulary of the Revolutionary War springs from that conflict's clashes of arms. A vocabulary alone, however, is meaningless—a babble of battles without a grammar to give it order. The grammar of war is strategy. Strategy provides a framework or context in which the battles can be logically examined. The first part of this text emphasizes the strategy employed by the rebelling colonists.

Strategy was not a word that George Washington used. It entered the language some years after his death. A military dictionary published in London in 1802 listed the term "strategem," but it was defined as simply a ruse, a gambit to gain surprise. A French manual of about the same time included the word "strategie," and defined it as movement beyond the enemy's visual circle or cannon range. That does not mean that strategy did not exist at this time, however. Although they did not articulate the term, the great and near great military leaders of history obviously understood and implemented the concept.

Writing after the Napoleonic Wars, the Prussian military philosopher, Carl von Clausewitz, defined strategy as "the use of engagements for the object of the war." As applied to the Revolutionary War, that means that the Patriot strategy was the course set by Washington—and the Continental Congress, at times—to attain the aims for which the colonies were fighting. One of those aims was independence. Patriots finally articulated it in a formal declaration after more than a year's fighting. The other major object was territorial aggrandizement. A successful strategy, therefore, had to leave the colonies free from foreign domination and also in control of the lands on their borders.

The formulation of a strategy is influenced by many factors. Two of the most important are enemy capabilities and intentions, and the geographic realities of the theater of war. Both of these factors had great influence on the kind of strategy that Washington could implement at any given time. Accordingly, as the first two chapters in the text stress, his strategy differed from period to period, thus giving rise to varying opinions of his generalship. That is to say, his "use of engagements" differed as external factors forced him to adjust his approach. Throughout the war, however, Washington held unswervingly to achieving the ends of the war, and never confused ends with means.

While the first two chapters in the text emphasize strategy and the campaigns that implemented that strategy, the last two chapters trace the evolution of American military policy in its early years. Three major themes are emphasized in these chapters. One of them is the story of how the early leaders created and relied upon two armies: a standing army of professional soldiers, and a citizen army of militia and volunteers. Another centers on the folly of unpreparedness and the use of inadequate military means in attempts to achieve overly ambitious ends. The third theme is associated with the beginning of professionalism in the Regular Army. Each of these themes either has roots in or an indirect relationship to the Revolutionary War, with which our narrative commences.

Independence Strains the Infant Nation's Capacity for Defense: 1775-1777

The American Revolutionary War did not begin suddenly—it developed slowly, over a period of more than a decade. Specifically, friction arose from three major areas of controversy: land, money, and the Royal Army. At the end of the French and Indian War, England decided to maintain a portion of the Royal Army in America. Some colonists pointed to the widespread belief that the King had sent precious little help when France had been a threat in the New World, and thus questioned the purpose of such a garrison in a period when no external danger was apparent. A bloody Indian uprising in 1763, led by Pontiac, chief of the Ottawa tribe, momentarily muted American murmurs about the need for an army. The redcoats remained. In an attempt to placate the tribes, a boundary was drawn along the Appalachians beyond which white men were barred. American settlers and land speculators were bitter. When landowners and squatters refused to comply with the new arrangement, soldiers bodily removed them from the forbidden country. Neither British law nor the King's soldiers gained in popularity.

The English treasury had been emptied; in fact, it had been forced far into debt by the heavy expenses of the Seven Years' War. King and Cabinet, searching for any course that might produce some revenue and knowing that the people in England were already taxed to the limit, turned not unnaturally to their colonies. It seemed only logical that the Americans—theretofore relatively free from taxation—should help defray the expense of their own defense. The Americans did not see it that way. They had not wanted British garrisons, and they most strongly objected to paying for them. Parliament passed a series of provisions—including the Currency Act, Sugar Act, Stamp Act, and tea tax—aimed at providing revenue. Infuriated Americans defied each and every decree. Inevitably, violence occurred. Resistance led to rioting, and rioting to bloodshed. In 1770,

martyrs were made in the "Boston Massacre."

Fired by hotheads such as Samuel Adams and Patrick Henry, tempers flared. Ships were sunk, tea destroyed, and Royal officials tarred and feathered. British troops were withdrawn from the frontier and massed in Boston, and the First Continental Congress voted a boycott of all English goods. The stage was set for a war that neither side wanted. Tact and diplomacy were called for. Unfortunately, George III, served by some of the most inept ministers in England's history, decided to compel obedience from his upstart subjects beyond the Atlantic by force of arms. No Englishman of stature really understood Americans or knew America.

Geographical realities shaped the course and conduct of the war in significant ways. It was a wild frontier country, very unlike the Europe of that day. Primordial forests covered most of the land. It was said that a squirrel could have travelled to every square mile in the colony of New York without once touching the ground. Roads were few and poor—hardly more than trails cut through the forests. One early law prescribed that no stump over one foot high could be left in a highway. It took seven days by carriage to journey from Philadelphia to West Point, a trip that takes a mere three hours by automobile today. Maneuver, therefore, was dominated by rivers—highways leading from the sea that were severe obstacles to movement on land. Probably the single most significant geographical factor associated with George III's rebellious American provinces was the sparseness of population. More people live today in the borough of Brooklyn than lived then in the entire 13 colonies. Totaling about two and a half million, the population was spread in a great 1,100-mile arc, stretching from Boston to Savannah. *(See Map 1.)* Cities were small. New York occupied only the southern tip of Manhattan Island. Just four towns (Boston, New York, Philadelphia, and Charleston) had populations of over 10,000, and each of

The Boston Massacre, March 5, 1770. Engraving by Paul Revere, 1770

those was on or near the sea. All in all, it was a harsh land, not suited to warfare as it was practiced in that age.

The Rebellion Commences

General Thomas Gage, commander of His Majesty's forces in America, was not happy with his lot in Boston. Aware of the danger inherent in attempting to enforce strong measures with a small army, he wanted reinforcements and wiser colonial policies from England. Instead, he received the order to use force.

British intelligence sources reported that there was a rebel supply cache in the nearby town of Concord. *(See Map 2a.)* Gage reasoned that a fast moving column could surprise the guards, destroy the stores, and return to Boston before the unorganized militia could react. A bungled beginning lost both time and the element of surprise for the British. The countryside was alarmed. Embers of revolt that had been smoldering for a decade burst into flame on April 19, 1775, when a small group of militiamen stood in the path of the British on Lexington Green. The clash at Lexington can scarcely be called a skirmish. Neither did a substantial fight occur at Concord. The real battle took place as the 1,800 raiders attempted to return to Boston.

All day long, as word of the English excursion spread from town to town, infuriated Yankees grabbed weapons and headed for Boston in a massive, spontaneous response to the affront. The redcoats' retreat soon became one long, continuous ambush. Hampered by a growing number of dead and wounded, the English quickly found their situation desperate. Stragglers were tomahawked, while the main body of troops was a slow, compact target for any farmer who could discharge a musket. Many could and did. Although their aim was abominable, so many men sent so many balls whistling into the red ranks that the effect was telling. Nearly squeezed to a halt, the bloodied column appeared doomed; only a rescue force sent by Gage from Boston saved it from annihilation.

The Battle of Lexington, 1775

Meeting in Philadelphia on May 10, 1775, the delegates to the Second Continental Congress were not especially pleased to discover a war in progress. The British in Boston were penned up by a clamorous army of individuals looking for a chance to shoot a "lobsterback." *(See Map 2a.)* Adding to the discomfiture of Congress, Benedict Arnold and Ethan Allen seized Ticonderoga, the great fort on Lake Champlain, on the same day that the delegates convened. New England brought its case to Philadelphia and asked for help. Continental representatives had no authority to assume responsibility for the mob in Massachusetts. Nor was Congress empowered to wage war. Despite these legalities, the exigencies of the situation demanded that some control be exercised. Reluctantly, Congress grasped the reins of rebellion.

Hoping against hope that hostilities would soon end in reconciliation with the mother country, Congress nonetheless took steps to guide the fighting. The throngs besieging Boston were adopted as the basis of a Continental Army, and some troops were recruited from other colonies. Then, in what might well have been its wisest decision of the war, Congress appointed one of its members, a planter from Virginia named George Washington, to the position of Commander-in-Chief. He quietly thanked his fellow legislators and departed for New England.

The Battle of Bunker Hill

Meanwhile, in Massachusetts the colonists continued to act in a belligerent manner, and for some obscure reason decided to occupy Charleston Peninsula. Having almost no artillery, there was little they could gain by holding that terrain, while they risked the complete loss of their force should the British cut across the peninsula's narrow neck. But hold it they were determined to do. Though no commander was appointed, William Prescott and Israel Putnam—two highly respected men of forceful character—assumed a sort of dual leadership. After dark, on June 16, troops with spades stole out onto the peninsula, passed Bunker Hill, by far the better defensive position, and began digging in on Breed's Hill. At daybreak they presented the surprised British with a *fait accompli*. Freshly turned earth marked a redoubt on the crest, and firing positions could be seen along a rail fence in the flat to the left of the hill.

Gage called a council of war to consider the situation. It has been said that councils of war do not fight, but this one was spoiling for a battle. Three major generals, all destined to achieve high command in the war, had just arrived from England and were eager to make a reputation: William

Sir William Howe

Howe, Henry Clinton, and John Burgoyne. They voted to assault the foolhardy rebels that very day—only the method of attack was a source of argument. Gage designated Howe to command the attacking force. Howe envisioned a secondary attack against the redoubt, while the main attack was to hit the American left at its junction with the Mystic River and then turn in to envelop the defenders on the hill. *(See Map 2b.)* He planned to take artillery with him, while warships would be employed to fire on the hostile flanks and to interdict the neck of the isthmus to prevent reinforcement from the mainland. With surprising speed, seldom matched again in the war by anyone in either army, Howe organized his command that morning, landed beneath the American lines shortly after midday, and formed for battle in the afternoon.

Those morning hours had not been wasted by the Americans. Their breastworks had been improved, and a strongpoint had been constructed precisely at the point Howe hoped to penetrate with his main attack. Perhaps 1,500 men crouched in their positions on Breed's Hill. That many or more were on Bunker Hill, to the rear. Thousands more watched from the mainland beyond the slender neck of the peninsula. Farmers preparing to do battle with European regulars, they were nervous. But veterans of the French and Indian War circulated among them with the advice, "Hold your fire until they are 100 feet away, aim low, and try to pick off the officers."

To begin the attack, Howe ordered his artillery forward to hammer the defenses. Embarrassed, the gunners reported that in the hasty movement they had brought 12-pound ammunition and 6-pound guns. Howe's comments were not recorded. Turning to his infantry, he signalled for an advance. The disciplined red ranks surged forward, a sobering sight to the apprehensive Patriots. With heels hitting in unison to the heavy drumbeat, muskets pointing uniformly skyward, and shoulders nearly touching, the men in the first rank marched in stately, stoic formation toward the waiting Americans. Two paces behind came another line. And another. File closers* formed a ragged fourth rank. British commanders watched proudly; in laudable precision, their men were displaying a classic example of eighteenth century linear tactics. At about 50 yards, as the English deployed for a bayonet charge, a blast of musketry cut the first ranks to pieces. Some of the King's men began a sporadic and ineffective return fire while their rear ranks moved forward, mingling with other units. Continuing to "aim low," Americans poured volley after volley into the confused redcoats, causing them to withdraw.

Flushed with victory, Putnam rode back to the mainland in a vain effort to bring up reinforcements. To his surprise and chagrin, few among those watching the fight cared to join it.

Within minutes, Howe reorganized and launched his second attack. *(See Map 2c.)* This time he sent a main attack against the redoubt, while a smaller force charged the rail fence to tie down the American left. Again, entrenched defenders waited until the last moment to open fire. Confident now, they delivered more efficient fire than before. The British ranks were stopped cold, and took heavy casualties. Under the deadly fusillade, they fell back a second time. Each British soldier was burdened with 100 pounds of equipment; physically spent by two attempts to clamber up the slope, he had nothing left for a third try. In nearly complete disarray, survivors flocked back to the beach. Some units had lost over three-fourths of their strength. All 12 members of Howe's personal staff were either dead or wounded.

The ecstatic Americans had suffered negligible losses. Still, the courageous troops on Breed's Hill could get no support. Pleading, cursing, threatening, and beating were to no avail; the sweating officers could not force militia units stationed around the bay to move forward. Short of powder but determined to win, the Patriots awaited another British attempt.

It came, but not before Howe had made some changes.

(See Map 2d.) He obtained 400 reinforcements, told all the men to drop their cumbersome packs, maneuvered artillery to enfilade the defenses—the proper ammunition had finally arrived—and ordered a bayonet charge. That third attempt succeeded, and the redcoats breached the breastworks. Out of powder and possessing no bayonets, the Americans withdrew to Bunker Hill, and then back to the mainland.

The battle had been costly. Of some 2,400 English engaged, over 1,100 were shot. Included in that number were 92 officers. In one regiment, just four men escaped unharmed; in another, only three. American casualties were 440, with most of those inflicted in the retreat.

Results were far-reaching. Americans came away with the impression that grit and guts were all one needed to be a soldier, while English officers were convinced that it was sheer folly to assault breastworks. Neither side correctly read the lessons of the battle, but the Americans' error was the more grievous—it would nearly cost them the war.

George Washington Takes Command

When Washington arrived in Massachusetts in July, he surveyed his army and was dismayed. About 17,000 strong, it was an army in name only. Lacking clothing, equipment, training, and discipline—in fact, just about everything except anger at the British—it was a true rabble. Molding an army was Washington's first task. He energetically began to create order out of chaos by establishing an administrative organization, shaping a command system, and starting a training program. A Continental Army was formed, but recruiting lagged, as local and state troops were intent on quitting as soon as their short tours were up. At best, the general's efforts were only partly successful.

Washington had another great problem. Perhaps more important than organizing the army was the necessity for retaining the initiative. Although the Continental Army was inadequately equipped and all but untrained, the enemy was also weak. Washington believed that the Patriots were obliged to exploit every opportunity for aggressive action, for, in time, reinforcements arriving from England could be anticipated. Boldness would have to substitute for experience, and spirit for resources. Audacity would be a virtue. On August 4, 1775, Washington wrote, "We are in a situation which requires us to run all risques." Boldness, he added, could bring success even to "enterprises which appear chimerical." Without a fleet, Washington could neither strike at the British-held islands in the West Indies

---

*File closers were non commissioned officers who fitted out the last rank of a formation.

Washington and Major General Artemus Ward Surveying Lines Before Boston, 1775

George Washington Equestrian Statue at West Point

nor deter the movement of British reinforcements. Therefore, he turned to the only British-controlled area that was within his reach—Canada.

The Invasion of Canada

The Canada that Congress hoped would become the "14th colony" could have been called a river with two towns. *(See Map 3.)* Except for scattered settlements along the St. Lawrence River, the vast reaches of that northern land were little touched by civilization. Montreal and Quebec were the key citadels along the waterway; Canada would stand or fall according to the fate of those two fortified river towns.

It was simple for the Patriots to select an avenue of invasion—the old military route of the Colonial Wars was too obvious to be overlooked. An army could travel from New York to Montreal via the Hudson River, Lakes George and Champlain, and the Sorel River, with only a minor portage or two between the Hudson and the lakes. In fact, Congress had already authorized such an attempt before Washington acted. General Philip Schuyler, an aristocrat from New York, was entrusted with command of the expedition.

Schuyler, however, was not enthusiastic. Preparations for the invasion lagged. Weeks passed, and the opportunity to seize Canada, then virtually defenseless, diminished before the onset of winter. In complete exasperation, General Richard Montgomery, Schuyler's deputy, gathered 1,200 men, loaded them onto a makeshift fleet, and set sail northward. Schuyler, from either infirmity or sloth, accepted the insubordinate actions of his hotheaded lieutenant and decided to support the operation. Having started late, the plucky force was soon stalled by British defenses at St. Johns, and lost most of September and October in working around General Guy Carleton's skillfully arranged positions. It was during that slow maneuvering that Ethan Allen, headstrong and impatient, attempted to capture Montreal with a handful of men. He was captured for his pains and shipped in chains to England.

Meanwhile, back in Cambridge, Washington was chafing over his inability to strike at the British, and growing increasingly frustrated by pessimistic reports from Schuyler. There was one other path to Canada: up the Kennebec River, across an arduous portage, and down the Chaudiere River. It was neither a well-known nor an easy route, but a determined force under a driving leader could make it. Colonel Benedict Arnold was such a leader, and Washington told him to go. The scheme offered the possibility that, through surprise, Quebec would be captured, thus turning the defenses of Montreal. It entailed a dangerous dispersal of forces, however, in that neither Arnold nor Montgomery would be strong enough to insure victory, while either or both could easily be totally defeated. Washington was taking great risks, but he stood to win great rewards.

In mid-September, Arnold and 1,100 men began their journey. The difficulties of making such a march had been completely underestimated, as the struggling soldiers soon learned. Boats, made hurriedly of green wood, leaked, spoiling food and ammunition. Constant immersion in cold water and exposure to chilling weather began to take a toll of men and morale. The rearguard commander deserted, taking 300 troops with him. For six weeks, Arnold pushed his ever-weakening column through swamps, around rapids, and down rock-filled streams. It rained most of the time, but snow and sleet fell too. During the last days of the march, the troops ate boiled moccasins. On November 2, food was finally obtained as the gaunt scarecrows staggered into civilization once more, reaching a French farming community. Perhaps half of the original number had survived.

On that same day, St. Johns fell and Montgomery pushed his undisciplined troops on toward Montreal. When they reached it, on the eleventh, Carleton decided not to make a stand. He made his escape in civilian clothes, and Montgomery occupied the city two days later.

Arnold, after permitting his men a short period to recuperate, pushed on to Quebec, reaching the river opposite the town on November 9. Within a day he had gathered enough boats to cross the river and assault the fortress, but he was turned back by a violent storm. On the thirteenth he shuttled across, only to discover that a reinforcement had reached the city on that very day, making the garrison too strong for Arnold's little band to assault. Washington's audacious plan had failed by a day.

Nevertheless, all Canada save Quebec was in American hands, and no British reinforcement could be expected until spring. Montgomery, having joined Arnold, assumed command of the combined forces. He had only to take his time and wait for severe weather, hunger, and disease to deliver Quebec to him. But waiting was the one thing he could not do; his troops had been enlisted for short terms, and their time was nearly up. He was obliged to stake everything on one assault. His plan was to attack in two columns, under the cover of darkness and bad weather, and to penetrate the weaker walls of the lower city. He hoped that Carleton would concentrate his troops in the main defenses. In a blinding snowstorm on the last day of 1775, the assault was launched. Arnold led one column, Montgomery the other. When Montgomery was killed in the first rush and Arnold

was wounded, the attack sputtered to a stop, and the defeated Patriots withdrew.

Arnold continued to lead the investment of the superior British garrison, but smallpox and short enlistments rapidly depleted his numbers. Reluctantly, the Americans retired. In the spring, when fresh units arrived from England, Carleton pushed the Patriots back into New York. The invasion was over. It had been a failure in every respect.

Courage, leadership, and sacrifice had not been lacking. Trying to do too much with too little could be cited as the primary reason for defeat, but the true cause was that America simply was not prepared for war. At the very top level, Congress had long vacillated before agreeing to prosecute the fighting forcefully. With the decision made belatedly, to invade Canada, bickering between colonies, jealousies among generals, and reliance on a militia system for manpower had combined to preclude the availability of sufficient troops. Even so, the small army might have accomplished the mission had it been disciplined and trained. It was not—and Canada did not become a part of the United States.

Patriot Success Leads to Independence

While Arnold and Montgomery were pursuing their Canadian adventure, Washington wrestled with the perplexing problem of ousting the British from Boston. An outright assault into the teeth of their formidable breastworks was out of the question. So, too, was an amphibious maneuver, for the Royal fleet held sway in the harbor. But Washington's desire to take the offensive was so strong that he carefully considered every imaginable course of action, no matter how slight the chance for success. He even seriously considered rushing the town over ice should the harbor freeze.

Regardless of his final plan, he would need cannon, an item conspicuously missing from his inventory. Someone remembered all the cannon at Fort Ticonderoga. The Commander-in-Chief turned to an energetic 25-year-old officer, Henry Knox. Appointing Knox Colonel of the virtually non-existent Continental Regiment of Artillery, Washington ordered him to bring his guns from Ticonderoga to Boston. Knox reached Ticonderoga early in December 1775, selected the cannon and mortars he would need, and put carpenters to work building sleds. With 80 yoke of oxen pulling some 42 sleds, Knox started his "noble train of artillery" on its epic journey in the deep snows of northern New York and New England. All told, he transported 59 weapons, with the largest mortars weighing approximately a ton each. By the end of January 1776, Washington had artillery.

The British Evacuation of Boston

In February, during a council of war, Americans thought of using artillery to goad the British into attacking a prepared position. Dorchester Heights was selected. *(See Map 2a.)* From there, artillery could sweep the harbor, forcing the British to either fight back or endure a galling cannonade. In an amazing display of Yankee ingenuity, the Patriots prefabricated their breastworks—the ground was frozen too hard to permit digging—and, in one night, carted a complete system of fortifications out to the heights. Barrels filled with earth, wooden frames crammed with bales of hay, and felled fruit trees formed an effective, if unusual, barricade. When the morning mist cleared on March 5, the astounded British estimated that between 12,000 and 20,000 men would have been required to do so much so quickly. Actually, about 2,000 men had done the job.

It soon became apparent that American guns could control the harbor, while British cannon could not be adequately elevated to return fire. According to the British naval commander, the rebel position would have to be eliminated, or His Majesty's Fleet would be obliged to quit the harbor. Howe, who had replaced Gage, quickly organized an assault force, but, deterred by a storm and perhaps recalling his fate at Bunker Hill, he cancelled the attack. Instead, he issued orders for the evacuation of Boston, taking his army and a horde of Loyalists to Nova Scotia.

British Repulsed in the South

Meanwhile, encouraged by reports that Loyalists in the southland would flock to the King's colors, authorities in London had arranged for an expedition to re-establish British control there. Henry Clinton, Howe's deputy, left Boston in January, before Howe had to evacuate that city. After considerable delay, Clinton rendezvoused with a fleet transporting troops from England, and attempted to capture Charleston, South Carolina. A mismanaged British attack, excellent work on the part of Colonel William Moultrie and his fellow defenders, and shifting shoals in the water approaches to the harbor led to a smashing success for the Patriots.

Independence Won

By the end of June 1776, the Americans had won their independence. Not a redcoat remained on American soil, and all thirteen colonies were firmly controlled by assemblies supporting the rebellion. A chain of victories, marred only by the repulse at Quebec, had preceded the English withdrawal. Many Americans had formed the impression that citizen-soldiers had been adequate for the task, and that throwing off the English yoke would be relatively easy. It was an impression that would die hard, and would pay very bitter dividends in the future.

Independence, as a cause, had been slow in coming. At first, the fighting cry had been against Parliament. George Washington had drunk toasts to the health of George III through most of 1775. Gradually, as the war continued and casualty figures climbed, feelings hardened. A call for independence, rather than redress of grievances, was heard more and more often. On July 2, 1776, Congress resolved that the United States were free and independent, verifying what men in arms had established on the battlefields.

Strategic Options

While English generals felt that their mission was to enter the royal colonies and throw out a renegade regime in order to restore lawful government, American generals defined their task as the defense of national shores against a foreign invader. Having won their independence, Americans would be obliged to defend it immediately. Each officer and soldier should now realize, Washington intoned solemnly in general orders announcing the Declaration of Independence "that the peace and safety of his Country depends (under God) solely on the success of our arms . . . ." If that was soldierly rhetoric meant to inspire the troops, it was also true. The new nation had no allies, no central executive authority, and no means to raise funds—in short, none of the trappings usually associated with national defense. Ultimate victory or defeat would depend purely on the performance of the thoroughly amateurish Continental Army and the still untried general at its head.

Earlier, a military defeat would have amounted to the quashing of a rebellion, and although it would have been a bitter pill for the Patriots to swallow, it would not have been fatal. Now, however, it could signal the death of the infant republic. Previously, Washington's primary goal had been the defeat of British forces; now his immediate objective was to prevent a decisive defeat of his own army. Nevertheless, his mission was to defend the United States, and he could not sacrifice any of the new states for the sake of saving the Army. He was expected to stand and fight, but it would have to be in a way that would allow him to disengage at any time in order to fight another day. Audacity and boldness had to bow to tenacity and shrewdness. There was a dilemma inherent in this new concept, however, and Washington quickly grasped it. If he fought, he could lose all; if he refused to fight, he could also lose all. As he stated at the time, every choice was fraught with difficulties.

Shortly after the Declaration of Independence, a new American strategy was devised to implement what Washington had already intuitively sensed was the proper course. At that time, Washington had the bulk of his army in New York, having begun moving forces there shortly after Howe evacuated Boston in the belief that New York might become the target for an English invasion. There, Washington hammered out the new strategy in a council of war with his leading generals. The council was strongly influenced by Major General **Nathanael Greene,** who argued that the outcome of the Revolution depended upon keeping an army in the field. That meant carefully avoiding a clash with the British that could become a Patriot disaster; the Americans, Greene stated, would need to take up positions "where the enemy will be obliged to fight us, and not us them." Following the council of war, Washington advised Congress of his new strategic concept. At least for the immediate future, he noted, the Americans must fight a defensive war, avoiding general actions that might risk too much and endanger the cause of the Patriots. It would have to be a war in which the safety of his army received paramount consideration—one in which the Americans did everything possible to protract the conflict in the hope of gaining strength and tiring the British. It was a fitting strategy for a weak force opposed by a powerful enemy. Even as the strategy was being formulated, the British were seizing a toehold in the vicinity of New York.

The British strategy for 1776 was formulated in a piecemeal fashion and after correspondence between officials in London and General Howe. Although a very few Englishmen doubted as early as mid-1775 that the British Army would ever be able to conquer America, there were many others who were busy proposing plans for snuffing out the rebellion. Those among them who were realistic about the situation fully understood that it was no longer a case of suppressing some rebellious colonial subjects; Howe's task now was to invade and conquer a hostile nation. To achieve this goal, the British had begun as early as the fall of 1775 to recruit sizable reinforcements for Howe's army, well before that soldier had withdrawn his small force to Halifax. Howe himself had been urging the Government to provide strong reinforcements so that he could engage the Americans in battle and inflict an overwhelming military defeat. Arguing that this needed to be done as soon as possible in order to convince the Americans of the futility of their rebellion, he also pointed out that the initiation of such a battle would not be easy, because the Patriots would melt away into the countryside and refuse to fight on terms favorable to the British. Moreover, if Howe's line of communication continued to consist only of the British fleet, the pursuit of Washington's force into the interior would be difficult, if not impossible.

Some officials in England proposed an alternative strategy—the occupation of several key seaports, accompanied by a naval blockade. From these safe enclaves, the adherents of this idea insisted, England could simply wait for the insurrection to wither on the vine as American commerce slowly strangled. The enclave idea, however, had obvious shortcomings, which knowlegeable men were quick to see. Numerous inlets and streams along the coastline made a blockade a dubious proposition, the initiative would rest with the Americans, the scheme would take too long to produce even questionable results, and the possession of the urban centers did not constitute a decisive objective. After all options had been examined, it appeared that Howe must occupy a base advantageous to the British and harmful to the Americans from which he would be able to force Washington into a decisive battle. Where should that base be?

The South was appealing. It was close to British forward bases in the West Indies, Loyalists were strong there, and reconquest of Georgia and the Carolinas would be relatively inexpensive and easy. In other words, the South was obtainable. But was it decisive? The heart of the rebellion was in New England, and it was not likely that northern rebels would lose their will to resist because of an English victory in southern states.

A move into Pennsylvania to capture Philadelphia was a possibility. Many Loyalists, Howe was assured, would rush to fight for the King. Taking the enemy's capital could also have a depressing impact on Patriot morale. Philadelphia would be an excellent base of operations. But operations to where? An attack against the South could be better supported from more southerly cities; a westward strike would hit nothing but scattered frontier settlements; and a push northward would be difficult in the extreme, since Washington would have all the defensive advantages of broad rivers and rugged mountains, not to mention more than enough space to permit him to avoid conclusive engagement.

Another course remained. New York City offered the best base of operations in America. Centrally located, easy to defend by a force with naval superiority, and blessed with an excellent harbor, it was an obvious choice. Moreover, it was the one place in the United States from which Howe could link up with other British forces in Canada. Taking and holding the line of the Hudson River would sever the rebellious states—separating New England from the rest—permitting the destruction of resistance in each half in turn.

Washington, as well as Howe, could easily determine the most promising location for an invasion. When the Royal Navy landed troops in the summer of 1776, a Patriot army was waiting for them.

The British Campaign of 1776

The army Howe began landing on undefended Staten Island on July 2, 1776 was to be the largest and best the British would ever assemble in America. It contained approximately 32,000 well-trained British and German regulars, all of whom were anxious to redeem professional prestige against the upstart Americans. Far to the north, Carleton, his army rested and reinforced, was poised to push south on Lake Champlain toward the upper Hudson. To oppose his foes, Washington had little more than a handful of survivors from the ill-fated Canadian invasion stationed around Ticonderoga, several half-completed forts in the Hudson Highlands near West Point, and his own army at the mouth of the Hudson. In July, local militia and Washington's regulars, the Continentals, marched and sailed down from Boston, providing him with a force in New York of nearly 10,000. Frantic appeals to Congress and nearby states brought in enough reinforcements to double the size if not the quality of the Patriot army before the British finally attacked in August. It was the largest force Washington had ever commanded, but, significantly, it was mostly untrained. By far, the greater part had not benefited from the discipline and instruction meted out in Boston. Washington was still plagued by the persistence on the part of Congress and the states in limiting enlistments to a few months, or a year at most.

Washington's worst strategic blunder of the war was his decision to defend the port of New York. *(See Map 4.)* Apparently, political pressure and a poor opinion of British generalship led him into the trap. But for British bumbling and that special providence which seemed so often to favor the Americans, the rebellion probably would have been snuffed out then and there, in 1776. The Patriots had no fleet, while the waters surrounding Manhattan and Long Island were choked with ships under the command of Admiral Lord Richard Howe, the general's brother. Kingsbridge, on the far northern tip of Manhattan, was the sole route of escape for the Continental Army. The harbor and

town of New York were critical objectives for the British, but there was no way in which the Americans could defend them. Had Howe elected to land above the American positions to sever their one slender link to safety, it is hard to see how Washington could have escaped annihilation. Howe was not a bold strategist, though. He settled for a more prosaic landing on Long Island, rather than a deep turning movement.

Washington decided that he must defend Brooklyn Heights on Long Island if he were to defend Manhattan. He therefore divided his army between the two places—a tactical error matching his strategic mistake in even being there, and another step toward disaster. For all practical purposes, command on Long Island itself was also divided. Greene was first given the assignment, but, when he became ill, Major General John Sullivan was chosen as Greene's replacement. Not completely satisfied with this arrangement, Washington at the last moment placed Major General Israel Putnam over Sullivan, but Putnam hardly had time to become acquainted with the situation and the terrain before the British struck. American forces on Long Island were disposed behind imposing fortifications on Brooklyn Heights and in forward positions along a line of thickly wooded hills running across the southern end of the island. Sullivan was in immediate command on the American left; Brigadier General William Alexander, also called Lord Stirling, was on the right. Four roads led through the hills into the Patriot positions. Sullivan, in violation of the principle of security, left the Jamaica-Bedford road unguarded. As luck would have it, Howe planned to send his main attack swinging down that very road.

On August 22, 1776, Howe landed on Long Island in force. Washington had hoped to draw him into a repeat performance of Bunker Hill, but this time Howe gave the Americans some painful, if soon forgotten, lessons in maneuver and surprise. His plan called for a secondary attack against Stirling on the American right and a simultaneous demonstration* on Sullivan's front. Then the main attack was to envelop Sullivan's left flank. Assisted admirably by the American failure to guard the Jamaica-Bedford Road, Howe's plan worked to perfection on August 27. The demonstration on Sullivan's front lured his forces out from behind their fortifications into the open, where they were crushed between columns. Though Stirling's Maryland and Delaware Continentals on the American right put up a valiant fight, it was a hopeless one; the rest of the American front crumpled as inexperienced

---

*A demonstration is a diversionary operation without actual physical engagement of troops that seeks to hold the enemy's attention and prevent his movement.

troops fled in terror before British and Hessian bayonets. The badly battered remnants fell back to entrenchments on Brooklyn Heights, fully expecting vicious pursuit from an enemy flushed with an easy victory.

One of the great mysteries of the Revolutionary War is why General Howe failed to follow up his success and launch a direct attack on the disorganized and panicky Americans on the Heights. Perhaps it was because he had bitter memories of Bunker Hill, or perhaps because he looked on the destruction of Washington's army as being of lesser import than the reconciliation of the country to British rule. In any case, he decided to seize the fortifications on the Heights by regular approaches in the traditionally accepted style of Vauban, a process that would require several days. That delay enabled the Americans to escape. (Ironically, Washington himself would employ the same technique over five years later to win the war at a Virginia town named Yorktown.)

Realizing that the position on Long Island was untenable and that at any moment the British fleet might sail up the East River and cut off his entire force, Washington ordered a withdrawal. Luckily, wind and weather held off British warships. Boats were collected from all available sources around New York City, and skilled fishermen from Colonel John Glover's Marblehead Regiment were assigned to operate them. Despite several incidents, each threatening disaster, the evacuation was successfully completed under cover of darkness on the night of August 29–30. Howe awakened the next morning to find that his quarry had escaped.

Having reconcentrated his forces in Manhattan, Washington deployed them at danger points stretching from New York City on the southern tip to Harlem Heights on the northern end. Garrisons in Fort Washington and Fort Lee guarded the Hudson on the New York and New Jersey shores respectively. But morale was now at a low ebb; militia began to leave by companies, and there was a high rate of desertion among the Continentals. Beyond this, the position of the whole army was still precarious, for the British clearly had the capability of landing on the New York mainland in Washington's rear and isolating his force on Manhattan Island.

Howe paused. In his pocket he carried tentative peace proposals from London. A year earlier the English terms offering pardon and conciliation might have been accepted. But independence had been declared. War aims had changed; freedom, not redress of grievances, was now the rallying cry of the rebels. Washington curtly sent Howe's emissary back with the observation that those who had committed no fault wanted no pardon. The non-productive and ill-advised British attempt to negotiate a peace treaty only served to give Washington a sorely needed breathing spell.

Howe's next move, on September 15, was not an advance onto the mainland to isolate Washington, but a landing in the center of Manhattan Island at Kip's Bay (the present site of 34th Street, but then well above the city). He hoped to save the town of New York, which was needed for winter quarters, and to lure Washington into decisive battle. Once again, Washington was in a position fraught with danger, and once more Howe tarried long enough to let him escape. The British advance guard received a check at Harlem Heights on September 16, and there the two armies faced each other for the better part of a month. At long last, when Howe launched amphibious landings to threaten the American escape route, the Commander-in-Chief ordered a withdrawal. Lethargically, Howe pursued the Patriots to White Plains, where he and Washington clashed briefly and inconclusively on October 28.

Meanwhile, on Lake Champlain, a wilderness arms race had been in progress. *(See Map 3.)* The British were at St. Johns building an armada to transport their army southward. Americans decided to counter that threat by constructing a fleet to strike at Carleton before he was fully prepared. An aggressive leader with a knowledge of seamanship was needed to turn back the northern prong of the Royal pincers; Benedict Arnold fit that description. Designated commander of all American forces on the lake, the irrepressible Arnold was an inspiring and energetic leader. What matter that there was nothing to command? He would build a fleet, recruit and train crews, and go to meet the enemy. Racing frantically against time, for Carleton had an earlier start, he succeeded.

On October 11, Arnold's outgunned and outmanned flotilla engaged the British near Valcour Island. Hammered by the superior fleet and harassed by Indians firing from the shore, Arnold conducted the battle with great verve and tenacity, if not with conventional naval tactics. His own vessel, *Congress*, was at the center of the fight as a constant example to the others. He himself limped about the deck shouting encouragement here, aiming a cannon there, barking orders above the din of battle, and inspiring the men to match his bravery. Both sides suffered severe loss and damage. Finally, after mutual exhaustion, the conflict ended in a draw. But the Americans were in no shape to engage again. Aided by dense fog and a dark night, Arnold slipped away to a station eight miles farther south. After making repairs and assessing his casualties, he decided to sail for Crown Point and protection. To shield the retreat of his disabled boats, the general-turned-admiral fought again. The statistic that 27 of the 73 crewmen aboard Arnold's command ship were killed or wounded attests to the heat of the struggle. His task finished—the enemy delayed—Arnold beached his razed, near-helpless hulks and burned them with flags flying.

Although defeated tactically, the bantam American "navy" had won a magnificent strategic victory. Carleton had been sorely weakened and decisively delayed. With winter near, the British general did not dare attempt further operations in the wilds of northern New York. He prudently retired to Canada.

After Washington withdrew from White Plains, Howe retraced his steps to capture bypassed Forts Washington and Lee. (The fortresses were located where George Washington Bridge now spans the Hudson.) Given that respite, Washington crossed into New Jersey and moved by stages toward the Delaware River, with Howe following. He had lost New York, suffered thousands of casualties, and been defeated at almost every turn. Throughout the campaign, contact between the two armies had been constant but, except for Long Island, not entangling. Nathanael Greene was one of many who marveled at the skill Washington displayed in managing "to skirmish with the enemy at all times and [yet] avoid a general engagement." An English officer, writing a personal letter, expressed his frustration with the Virginian's strategy: "As we go forward into the country the rebels fly before us, and when we come back they always follow us. 'Tis almost impossible to catch them. They will neither fight nor totally run away, but they keep at such a distance that we are always a day's march from them. We seem to be playing at bo peep." It was during this period that British officers began calling the rebel leader "the Old Fox"—a derisive term when they were chasing him, an admiring one when he proved too slippery to catch.

Seldom would the Patriot cause appear so hopeless, or would faith flicker so low. But all was not lost. Washington, a weaker but wiser general, had an army still in the field. Moreover, largely due to the exploits of Benedict Arnold, the Hudson was yet under American control. By failing either to destroy the rebel army or to isolate New England, the British had left a spark of resistance—a spark that Washington would be quick to fan.

The Christmas Campaign

The winter that Napoleon Bonaparte was a 7-year-old schoolboy and Frederick the Great, at 64, was in the twilight of his life, George Washington conducted a startlingly brilliant campaign which ranks with the best of Frederick's past accomplishments and Napoleon's future exploits. Had he done nothing before or after, Washington's 10 days from December 25, 1776 to January 4, 1777, would alone place

him high on the list of history's outstanding generals.

When Washington gathered his scattered and battered army in a position of temporary security beyond the Delaware River, even he was sorely surprised by his force's small size and sorry state. "Pitiful" was a description often used—and properly. Many men had no shoes, all were in rags, and few had retained such equipment as they had been issued. The winter had been mild so far, and that had saved them, but such luck could not last. Despair was prevalent, among the officers as well as the troops. Defeatism took over. It should be remembered, however, that an army is never beaten until it thinks it is, and one man, at least, refused to acknowledge defeat—the Commander-in-Chief, George Washington. He resolved to take offensive action against the overconfident British and Hessians as soon as possible. True enough, the Continental Army was now just a small fraction of its original size, but those left were the ones who counted. They had remained loyal and staunch. They were the hardcore rebels. They were winter Patriots; not a sunshine soldier was among them.

Banking on achieving surprise, Washington planned to cross the broad Delaware in three columns. *(See Map 5c.)* General James Ewing was to cross with militia south of Trenton to block the enemy escape route in that direction, while Washington personally would lead his Continentals in the main attack across the river above Trenton to fall on the garrison from the north. The third force, comprised of some militia troops under the command of Colonel John Cadwalader, was to cross near Bordentown in a diversionary operation. After Trenton was taken, Washington envisioned a rapid stroke with his united army against the garrisons of the well-stocked depots at Princeton and Brunswick. He selected Christmas Day for the attack.

When the three columns approached the river at nightfall, prospects looked dim. The current was unusually swift, temperatures had dropped alarmingly, and a fierce winter storm was brewing. Ewing's column took a long look and turned back. Cadwalader crossed some of his men to the opposite shore, but, when the storm struck, lashing the areas with high winds and soaking and chilling the men with alternating rain and snow, he withdrew them. Washington drove his column over the treacherous river in spite of the elements. When informed that rain and river water had ruined most of the powder, he shrugged off the bad news and, firmly displaying an iron resolve, ordered that Trenton be taken at bayonet point.

In Trenton, a quiet river town garrisoned by 1,200 Hessians of Colonel Johann Rall's Brigade, security was lax, even though local Tories and American deserters had reported the exact time and place of Washington's attack. *(See Map 5a.)* Rall, a heavy drinker who was contemptuous

The Battle of Trenton, December 1776

of Americans and their laughable army, had been commended several times for bravery, but never for intelligence. As dawn broke on the twenty-sixth, Rall was sleeping off a glorious alcoholic binge while his brigade was innocent of its impending doom. When Washington's veterans smashed into the sleepy town, surprise was complete and stunning. Flabbergasted Hessians tried to form in the streets, but were cut down by grape from the guns of Knox's Continental Artillery, notably those commanded by Captain Alexander Hamilton. Attempting to rally around four of their own cannon, the Germans were driven off by American flanking fire and a wild charge that captured the four guns. Lieutenant James Monroe was wounded while leading a rush on one of the artillery pieces. From then on it was a matter of mopping up with bayonet. Many of the terror-stricken Hessians fled southward and escaped, but over 100 were killed or wounded, and almost 1,000 were captured. Not a single Continental was killed, and only four were wounded.

Saddled with his prisoners, and aware that his other two columns had failed, Washington reluctantly decided to return to Pennsylvania. Attesting to the physical torture the Americans were enduring, two or three froze to death in the boats on the way back. By noon of the twenty-seventh, Washington's command, weak from two sleepless days and nights in dreadful weather, was back where it had started, but with the vital difference that victory had lifted its confidence.

Ashamed when he learned that Washington had pushed over the river, Cadwalader returned and crossed to the New Jersey shore on the twenty-seventh, the very day Washington completed his withdrawal! Finding that the British had evacuated their forward positions along the river after the Trenton fiasco, he quickly informed Washington. The Commander-in-Chief was in a quandary. Enlistments for the bulk of his men expired on December 31, and it would be the thirtieth before he could get back to New Jersey. He saw no way to conduct any kind of sustained operations.

It was then that Washington's natural aggressiveness—some might call it his gambler's instinct—asserted itself.

14

Feeling confidence in both himself and his men, he calmly crossed the Delaware for the third time on December 30. Once over, he turned recruiting officer. His Virginians would stay, and—for a $10 bonus—many New England soldiers extended their tours for six weeks. Other officers were able to enlist a few men from Pennsylvania and New Jersey. Washington started 1777 with a grand army of 1,600 veterans, most of whom had volunteered to stick by him. Assured of an army, for a while at least, he turned his attention once more to the enemy.

It was none too soon. General Charles Cornwallis was hurrying a strong column of redcoats toward Trenton. *(See Map 5b.)* Washington, needing time to mass his units, sent a delaying element up the road to Princeton. The delaying action was well conducted, obliging Cornwallis to deploy several times along the way, and keeping him away from Trenton until late on January 2. By then, the Americans were massed south of Assunpink Creek. Knowing that he could be overpowered by Cornwallis if he remained there, Washington marched away that night, leaving campfires burning. The old trick worked, and he was a day's march away when Cornwallis awakened on the third. More importantly, he had marched into New Jersey, cutting Cornwallis' line of communication at Princeton.

Washington's plan for falling on Princeton as he had Trenton was spoiled when an English unit, marching at dawn on the third. to reinforce Cornwallis, ran into the Americans just west of the town. In the fierce and confused battle resulting from that encounter, the Americans won due to the presence and leadership of Washington. When the Patriots showed signs of breaking, the Commander-in-Chief rode into their midst, rallied them, and cooly led a charge against the newly formed English position. Some 30 yards from the enemy muskets he stopped, turned his back on the hostile line, and commanded his troops to fire. That broke the British. Some Royal soldiers attempted a defense from the college area, but Alexander Hamilton's artillery changed their minds. Princeton was won.

Brunswick, with its huge and valuable supply cache, was just up the road. But Washington's men were absolutely on their last legs; he could depend on them no more. However, if he could not meet the British tactically, he would beat them strategically. *(See Map 5c.)* Quitting Princeton at almost the same moment that Cornwallis' panting advance guard entered from the south, the Americans marched to Morristown. That location was a perfect flanking position. From there Washington could threaten any British movement across New Jersey while wooded mountains protected him against Howe's forces. Valleys to his rear, running from southwest to northeast, provided him with a protected route stretching from the Hudson River almost to Phila-delphia, assuring the maintenance of his own line of communication. Howe, bowing to the inevitable, withdrew to New York. Washington ordered his haggard men into winter quarters as the flustered British evacuated New Jersey.

In the short space of 10 days, with a demoralized army that had been expected shortly to disintegrate, Washington had won two victories, had eluded a much larger force, had obliged the British to give up most of New Jersey, and had kept an army in the field. Patriot morale soared. The Revolution had been reduced to a single thread, but that thread had held.

A Professional Army Begins to Form

After two inconclusive years of fighting, it was painfully obvious to the Americans that victory would come neither quickly nor cheaply—if it came at all. As Washington had maintained almost from the start, the new nation could no longer attempt to wage war by the month. Planning and organization had to be for the long haul, the duration. In the midst of the crisis prior to Washington's victorious Christmas Campaign, Congress, demonstrating the amount of respect its army had earned, fled Philadelphia to safety. When they left, they endowed the Commander-in-Chief with temporary but extraordinary powers, which gave him for the first time a rather free hand. Those so-called "dictatorial powers" enabled him to start raising a real army during the winter at Morristown. But still it was only a start. An army is not just willed into being; it is built. And that takes time.

Enough men were enlisted for three years or the duration to give the Continental Army a dependable nucleus of veterans, but never were there as many as were needed. When Washington took the field in May 1777, he had only 8,000 troops; he was authorized nearly 10 times that many. The old practice of supplementing Continentals with militia would have to continue. The problem of securing and keeping good officers was also acute. Many were embittered by appointments and promotions made by Congress and the states, with more weight given to political influence than to military ability. Practically all found their pay inadequate in view of the runaway inflation. Too many able men resigned. Others, like Benedict Arnold, nursed grudges.

A brighter spot in the picture was the arrival of military supplies from France. The French court had been carefully watching the revolt in America. Louis XVI and his advisors were seeking an opportunity to redress the balance of power in Europe so heavily tipped in England's favor by her victory in the Seven Years' War. In 1776, Congress had sent a mission to France to seek supplies and financial aid, and to sound out the French on the possibility of entering the war on the American side. French ministers preferred to move with caution, awaiting some proof of the ability and determination of the United States to resist, but they did agree to the secret dispatch of military equipment under the guise of a commercial transaction. Supplies arriving in early 1777 were the beginning of what was to be a continuous flow. The French Charleville musket, an improved flintlock superior in some respects to the English "Brown Bess," eventually became almost the standard arm of the Continental infantry.

All in all, a most important first step had been taken toward raising, training, and equipping a stable force. One more season of campaigning and another bitter winter's work would be needed to complete the task.

The Campaign of 1777

In the winter months of 1776–1777, packets plowed the rough seas between London and New York as a campaign plan for 1777 was devised. Failure to win in 1776, and the galling episode in New Jersey at Christmastime, made British officials determined to end the insurrection with one grand blow in the coming year. Again, attention was focused on the Hudson River. Although the plan itself underwent some surprising and confusing changes, the British concept of operations was first to isolate New England by taking the line of the Hudson, and then to destroy that area, the "heart of rebellion." That concept was good. In fact, it might have been the only one that could have brought victory to England. Dreamed up by General John Burgoyne and Lord Germain in London, with suggestions from Howe, the plan to accomplish that mission was another matter. *(See Map 6.)* It called for a concentric advance of three columns on Albany. One force would attack south over the Lake Champlain route, a second would move down the Mohawk River from the west, and a third would strike up the Hudson from New York. Once they were combined, New England would be invaded from the vulnerable west.

The plan carried several obvious seeds of disaster:

1. It set up a split command, with no overall commander designated until the columns met at Albany.
2. Permissive and vague orders were issued to the separate commanders, giving them leave to alter the overall plan.
3. None of the three columns were within supporting distance of each other.
4. A concentric advance is hard to coordinate under the best of circumstances, and it was nigh impossible in the forests of eighteenth century North America.
5. Strength was dissipated in three columns.

A poor plan often works if it is boldly and expertly executed. This particular poor plan was to be as poorly executed.

At first, all went well. Burgoyne made excellent headway from Canada to Ticonderoga, and neatly maneuvered the Americans out of that important fortress. Lieutenant Colonel Barry St. Leger had immediate success with his composite force of Indians and redcoats streaming down the Mohawk. Howe, poised in New York, had Washington guessing as to his intentions. Then the plan fell apart.

For reasons known only to himself, Howe decided to attack the American capital city of Philadelphia. He moved to Chesapeake Bay by sea, while Washington scurried overland to intercept him. Because Howe had left just a small defensive garrison in New York, Washington took a calculated risk and left only a minimal force in the all-important Hudson Highlands fortifications. While Washington and Howe jockeyed for position in Pennsylvania, Burgoyne was having troubles in the north. Overconfident, he had decided to proceed from Ticonderoga by land, rather than by Lake George. That was a mistake. The few Patriots, commanded by Philip Schuyler, were able to make the thick north woods an ally. Felling trees in the road, building roadblocks of boulders, digging out fords, and taking pot shots from the forest, the Americans slowed Burgoyne. Partly it was his own fault; he insisted on travelling on campaign as a gentleman, with an extensive baggage train of niceties, including a mistress.

Meanwhile, St. Leger had been forced to flee by Benedict Arnold and a half-idiot. Schuyler, while blocking Burgoyne, had chosen to dispatch a fast-moving expedition up the Mohawk in an attempt to blunt that arm of the British attack. When no brigadier general would volunteer for the hazardous mission, Major General Arnold stepped forth. His troops consisted of a thousand men, including the half-idiot, Hon Yost. Having learned that the Indians held Yost in awe as some sort of supernatural being, the ingenious general employed his assistant to dupe the hostile Indians into precipitate flight. The English, thus abandoned, soon followed their allies.

More a hero than ever, Arnold returned to the main army above Albany to find a new commander and a changed sit-

Benedict Arnold

uation. Major General Horatio Gates, as ambitious as he was inept, had replaced Schuyler, while Burgoyne, though closer to the Hudson, was no longer confident of victory. ''Gentleman Johnny'' had lost a detachment at Bennington and was despairing of receiving assistance from the depleted garrison in New York. More importantly, militia reinforcements had swelled the American ranks to the point that a heavy numerical superiority had **been** achieved over the weakened invaders. Thaddeus Kosciuszko, a Polish military engineer who had come to America to assist the new nation, was on hand to direct the preparation of the Patriot entrenchments, while a survivor of the march to Quebec, Colonel Daniel Morgan, had brought in his riflemen to bolster the American lines. Arnold was given command of the left wing. On September 19, an indecisive battle was fought at Freeman's Farm. Arnold and Gates argued heatedly over the conduct of the conflict, with the result that Arnold was removed from command. The passionate but petty quarrel earned respect for neither officer.

Burgoyne was desperate. His supplies were all but gone, and his line of retreat had been cut. Hoping against hope for some action from New York City toward the Hudson Highlands, he resolved to gamble everything on one last assault

of the entrenched rebels. On October 7 he initiated the Battle of Bemis Heights. *(See Map 6.)*

When the two armies clashed, Gates, who would fail dismally three years later at Camden, was in a safe position two miles to the rear; Arnold, who would disappoint Washington three years later at West Point, was brooding in a tent. As the fighting raged, Arnold seethed. Finally, maddened by frustration and the scent of gunpowder, he leaped onto his brown mare, brandished his sword, and galloped to the smoke and sound of the guns. The British advance had already been checked. Although a Patriot counterattack at that stage could turn a mere tactical victory into a strategic success, Gates' plans were solely defensive. Moreover, from his haven far to the rear, that commander was unable to direct an offensive. At that critical moment, Benedict Arnold reached the front. It has been variously suggested that he was drunk, or had taken opium, or was momentarily insane, or simply wished to die. Explanations for his astounding actions are beside the point; it suffices to state the facts. Had the award been in existence then, it is safe to assume that Arnold would have earned the Medal of Honor for his work that day.

Charging to the head of one brigade, Arnold urged an attack against the Hessians opposing them. He had neither command nor authority, but no one dared question the wild-eyed, screeching general. The Patriots responded, and the Germans retreated. Burgoyne then attempted to withdraw all his units. He was not to escape so easily. Arnold, intent on driving in for the kill, found two more brigades and threw them against the center of the English position. Then, after miraculously escaping harm while traversing the entire field between the opposing lines, he led a violent and victorious assault on a fortified band of Canadians. Looking around for more troops to lead, he spied Morgan's riflemen. Placing himself in front of the frontiersmen, the magnificent warrior led his last charge in the uniform of the United States. As he crashed into the enemy barricades, a volley felled his horse, and a musketball smashed the bone in the same leg that had been hit at Quebec. Arnold and the sun fell together. Darkness and the loss of their leader stalled the American surge. Burgoyne was permitted to extricate his battered army, but his troops had been punished beyond recovery. A few days later he surrendered his entire command at Saratoga.

If the ball that shortened Benedict Arnold's left leg had entered his heart instead, he would be remembered today as one of America's greatest heroes. As it was, he lived to become one of its greatest villains.

To the south, Howe was having a rugged time getting to Philadelphia. By the time he landed, Washington was waiting. Moreover, the Delaware River, which led to the capital,

The Wounding of Benedict Arnold at Bemis Heights, October 1777

was blocked by forts and obstructions. Howe had to move overland.

The two armies clashed at the Battle of Brandywine on September 11. *(See Map 7.)* Washington took up a defensive position behind Brandywine Creek, and waited. In a beautifully executed maneuver, Howe launched a secondary attack against the left half of the Patriot position while enveloping their right. That move, abetted by abominable American intelligence work, caught Washington flatfooted. It was a repeat of the action on Long Island. Mixed elements, led by General John Sullivan, were hastily thrown into the teeth of the British assault. Sullivan, who had been captured at Long Island and might have seen history repeating itself had he had time to think about it, fought a frantic covering action, repeatedly plugging holes while slowly giving ground. The Americans, encouraged by the sight of the Commander-in-Chief himself riding up and down the lines, battled furiously. Their valiant action permitted the safe extrication of the bulk of the Patriot force. As it was, Washington lost over 10 percent of his men and 11 guns, but it could have been much worse.

In the following weeks, Howe called the tune and Washington danced. In a series of clever feints and jabs, Howe outmaneuvered Washington, took Philadelphia, destroyed much of a division, and captured significant quantities of supplies. It was a humiliating experience for Americans in

general, and for Washington in particular. He had failed in New York as a defensive fighter, and had done no better here. He decided to counterattack.

On October 4, just three days before Burgoyne launched his desperate attack at Bemis Heights, Washington assaulted the British position at Germantown. His plan was too complicated for the still untrained Continentals; four columns, spread over seven miles, were to have made a night march to concentrate on the battlefield. In fact, it would have been most difficult for even the automatons of Frederick the Great. Nevertheless, the Americans made an amazingly good show of it. Fog, confusion, and stout British resistance caused the attack to fail, but the important thing was that the men, the officers, and even the Commander-in-Chief looked upon it as a victory. Morale was raised, and Washington's prestige rose with it.

One other battle occurred in those climactic four days in October. As Howe was endeavoring to take Philadelphia and Burgoyne was laboring on the path to Saratoga, General Henry Clinton fretted in New York City with a small defensive force. In late September, reinforcements arrived, and Clinton resolved to make an attempt on the Hudson Highlands. Burgoyne was by then floundering badly. Clinton, unsure of being able to break through the Highlands defenses, planned only to create a diversion to the rear of the forces under Gates.

Departing from New York City on October 3, Clinton deposited a portion of his 3,000 British, Hessian, and Loyalist troops at Verplanck's Point two days later. *(See Map 8.)* The few Americans, protected by light breastworks and possessing but two cannon, fled at the approach of the landing party. The British bait had been swallowed. Major General Israel Putnam, the inept and elderly American commander, was convinced that Peekskill was the objective of the redcoats. So sure was he, in fact, that he ordered 50 men from Forts Montgomery and Clinton to reinforce the area near Anthony's Nose, thus further weakening the already undermanned fortifications. Having by that feint fooled Putnam, Clinton went ashore with the bulk of his forces early the following morning at Stony Point. A heavy fog covered the operations and delayed the Patriots' discovery that the English were on the western shore.

Led by a local Loyalist, the King's men began a fatiguing march to envelop the forts. Passing through defiles so narrow only three men could march abreast, and struggling up nearly vertical cliffs, the attacking force was unopposed in its difficult, day-long approach. As the hours wore on, General George Clinton, Governor of New York and cousin of Henry Clinton, realized that the main attack was aimed at his twin forts, Montgomery and Clinton. He appealed to General Putnam for aid, while sending light forces from the forts to delay the British advance. Henry Clinton, meanwhile, had reached Bear Mountain. Dividing his column, he sent one part on a circuitous route west of Bear Mountain to attack Fort Montgomery, while the second group was directed to assault Fort Clinton. The Americans who had been dispatched to slow the English arrived too late and were too few in number; they were quickly beaten back into the protection of the forts. As evening approached, the two English columns fixed bayonets and assaulted simultaneously. After a brief but spirited defense, both forts fell. Most of the defenders took advantage of the darkness and the rugged terrain to escape.

The opening of the remainder of the Hudson defenses proved to be easy. *(See Map 9.)* With the twin forts in British hands, the fleet was unimpeded in removing the water obstacles and sailing to Constitution Island. Manned by soldiers and convicts, American vessels floundered helplessly and were finally burned to preclude capture. Except for firing on the flag sent to demand capitulation, the garrison at Fort Constitution made no stand. Realizing, as some men had long before, that the dominance of the unoccupied land of West Point made their position untenable, the defenders destroyed the buildings and withdrew. On the eighth of October, Clinton sent an exultant letter notifying Burgoyne that help was on the way.

It was too late, however. The Royal flotilla ranged nearly to Albany, destroying much property along the Hudson's shores as it passed, before learning of Burgoyne's surrender. Clinton then destroyed the Patriot works in the Highlands and retired to New York. Howe went into winter quarters in Philadelphia. Washington took his army into nearby Valley Forge to watch Howe and to complete the training job begun the preceding winter.

The Campaign of 1777 had been an utter failure for England. Philadelphia had been taken, true, but Washington's moral victory at Germantown had impressed Europe more than his defeats had. Additionally, the loss of Burgoyne's entire army at Saratoga had astounded everyone. British prestige was shattered. Ragged, untrained Americans had defeated European regulars in a campaign that had been billed by England as the one to end the war. It was a decisive point in the war and in history. France, followed eventually by Spain and the Netherlands, sided against England, and the American war became a worldwide conflict. From that time on, it was to be a different war—one that the United States could hardly lose if Washington was able to keep a strong army together and avoid a major catastrophe. Nevertheless, it was one that would prove most difficult to win.

Allied Victory 1778-1781

2

When news of the astounding American victory at Saratoga and the sturdy performance of Patriot forces in Pennsylvania reached Paris, the effect was electrifying. For years, France had been seeking revenge for the humiliating drubbing England and Prussia had administered in the Seven Years' War. Her military arms had been refurbished in anticipation of the day of reckoning, and diplomats had eagerly read every sign to discern the right moment to strike. This was it. Paris, with some help from Madrid, had for some time been surreptitiously sending aid to the Americans. Now French leaders openly signalled support by signing a treaty of alliance with the United States on February 6, 1778. The war abruptly entered a new and ultimately decisive period. It had become a coalition war against England to be fought out on a much wider stage.

Just as the second phase of the Revolution (July 1776-1777) had presented Washington with a set of conditions wholly different from the first, so was this third one completely unlike either of the previous two. France's entry into the war added international legitimacy to the Revolutionary cause, assured a continuing source of supply, and held forth the promise of reinforcement by a French expeditionary army. But, important as those considerations were, they were surpassed in significance by one key factor: the introduction into the fray of the French Navy. Henceforth, there would be a fleet to challenge British supremacy in North American waters. France had been energetically regenerating her naval arm ever since the last war, while England had allowed her Navy to atrophy. In weight of guns and number of warships, the French were stronger. Britannia would not rule the waves uncontested. No longer would English generals have the privilege of freely shifting units along the Atlantic seaboard; no longer would they enjoy the unopposed strategic advantage of interior lines. The only advantage in mobility they had ever held over the Americans was thus endangered—if not altogether lost.

Because of the support of the French Navy, the entire thrust of Washington's strategy could now be reversed. Whereas he had been limited to acting on the strategic defensive as long as Great Britain had absolute superiority at sea, the arrival of a French fleet—or even the threat of its arrival—would permit him once again to pass over to the offensive. Military victory became possible. The invaders could be decisively beaten and driven off American soil. Patriots could accept greater risks, for now the loss of a major portion of the Continental Army would not necessarily be fatal; the Revolution had taken too firm a hold in the country to be rooted out by an England at war also with France. This is not to say that Americans could become foolhardy, but only that they could operate with less constraint, more daring. Seizing the initiative was Washington's new imperative; defeating the British forces was his overriding goal. The predominant theme motivating American activities during the four years between Saratoga and Yorktown would be the burning desire to smite the foe. In Washington's words, American actions were shaped by the need to make "one great vigorous effort at all hazards" to win the war. Long before that could occur, however, Washington and his troops had another vigorous winter to endure while the training process continued.

Readying American Forces and Defenses

Valley Forge and Foreign Advisors

Valley Forge has become a symbol of the suffering, devotion, and patriotism of those gallant men who overcame all obstacles to win America's independence. It was indeed a terrible time for the underfed, ill-clothed, poorly paid Continentals, but it was not the worst winter they endured, nor was mere survival their greatest accomplishment. When Washington marched his gaunt columns forth in 1778, he led an experienced and trained organization that was the equal or the better of its foe in almost every respect. He had built an army.

The dedication, energy, and desire of American amateur officers had not been enough to fashion a truly effective fighting force. Professional knowledge had been needed as well. Earlier in the war, Congress had sent agents to Europe to find and hire foreign officers to serve as advisors and commanders in the Continental Army. The response was greater than either Congress or Washington had imagined or wanted. They were swamped by a veritable deluge of foreign adventurers, soldiers of fortune, and officers bored with the peaceful situation in Europe. Although there were problems in dealing with so many Europeans clamoring to be high ranking American officers, a large number were accepted and granted commissions. The names of but a few will suffice to remind us of the very major role they played in the Revolutionary War: Marquis de Lafayette, Johann de Kalb, Thaddeus Kosciuszko, Louis Lebégue Duportail, Augustus H. F. von Steuben, and Count Casimir Pulaski. The revitalized army that left Valley Forge bore their imprint. Of greatest significance was the contribution of Steuben. He personally adapted European drills to American realities, wrote the drill manuals, and colorfully, if profanely, taught the soldiers.

West Point

While Steuben was drilling the Army into shape at Valley Forge, Kosciuszko was building an impregnable fortress at West Point. (*See Map 9.*) Washington, who had always thought that the loss of the Hudson River would be fatal to the cause, had been thoroughly frightened when the Highlands' defenses, on which the Patriots had lavished nearly three years of effort and untold treasure, had fallen so easily. As a matter of first priority, he directed that new and better fortifications be erected.

In the deep snows of January 1778, soldiers crossed the ice from Constitution Island and began raising works on the promontory known as West Point. Although it had been mentioned several times as a possible site for a fort, it had surprisingly been neglected by the inexperienced engineers charged with blocking the Hudson River. Remembering that the earlier forts near Bear Mountain had been rushed from the rear, the Patriots placed a series of mutually supporting forts and redoubts among the hills that lay to the

Contemporary Sketch of a Wooden Redoubt at West Point

Contemporary Sketch of a Battery Site at West Point

west of the level plain at West Point. On the plain itself, they erected a strong bastion overlooking the river. A large cast iron chain, protected by batteries at water level, was stretched from the rocks of West Point to Constitution Island. When it was completed in 1779, the fortress was almost certainly too formidable for whatever force the British could have thrown against it. They tried to buy the post from Benedict Arnold in 1780, but never attempted an assault.

England on the Defensive: 1778

Discovering itself at war with the French as well as the Americans, England decided to assume the strategic defensive in America during 1778, while concentrating in Europe. In accordance with that decision, General Henry Clinton, who had replaced the hapless Howe, decided to consolidate his own scattered forces in New York. Philadelphia, which had been taken at a high price in 1777, was to be evacuated. Partly out of fear of meeting a French fleet, Clinton proposed to send only heavy equipment, the sick, and some 300 Tories by sea, while his army was to march northward across New Jersey. Slowed by excessive baggage, a strong but sluggish artillery train, and burnt bridges, the British set out for New York in mid-June.

With a speed which would not have been possible the previous year, Washington sent his troops in pursuit. The Commander-in-Chief intended to seize the excellent opportunity before him. The British, marching in column and heavily encumbered, were separated from their fleet and

Washington Arrives at the Battle of Monmouth, June 1778

temporarily vulnerable. Most of Washington's generals were eager for a fight, but Charles Lee, Washington's second in command, advised against it. He argued that since ultimate victory was assured now that France was in the war, there was no need to engage in battle and risk repulse. Lee had been a British officer prior to the war, and was respected for his supposed skill in military matters. Washington called a council of war, which voted to avoid a general engagement while continuing to seek an opening on the enemy flank and rear. For a while, the Commander-in-Chief abided by the council's decision. However, when he learned that Clinton was en route to Monmouth Court House, and was therefore near enough for the Continentals to attack, he could no longer contain himself. Washington hurriedly sent Lafayette with a strong advance party to intercept the British, while he himself moved the main body forward. At that moment, Charles Lee changed his mind and demanded to be placed in command of the advance guard. Washington, very reluctantly, agreed that the post belonged to the second in command. With that decision, he lost his opportunity for a victory at Monmouth.

When Lee's 5,000 men reached Monmouth on June 28, Clinton faced him with a small but vigorously led covering force. Lee, the general who had not wanted to fight in the first place, lost control of his units, and a confused retreat covering about three miles followed. Washington, riding to the sound of battle, arrived, assumed command, rallied the troops, and stopped the British advance. Clinton, reinforced, launched several attacks, but was turned back each time by the disciplined and steady Americans. By nightfall, both sides were exhausted. It had been an unusually hot day, and a large percentage of the dead had been killed by sunstroke. Clinton escaped that night and reached the safety of Sandy Hook, having lost some 2,000 men, but having saved the army. American casualties totalled 230 dead and wounded.

The Continental Army had fought well and, after Washington relieved Lee, it had been superbly led. Although the Battle of Monmouth could be called a victory for neither side, it marked a turning point in the war. Henceforth, Continentals and redcoats would fight on even terms.

After the British had been in New York for less than a week, a large French fleet under the command of Admiral Charles Henri Theodat D'Estaing arrived off the harbor. Washington hoped they would attack and destroy the smaller English fleet, thus leaving British soldiers in New York at his mercy. The new alliance with France was due for a rocky start, however. D'Estaing, to the bitter chagrin of the Americans, decided not to risk his fleet in the harbor. Instead, a joint attack in August on the small British gar-

rison in Newport, Rhode Island, was agreed upon. That entire affair was abortive. General John Sullivan, commanding American troops there, antagonized the sensitive French aristocrats with his abrupt manner. Washington sent Lafayette to smooth ruffled feathers and to act as liaison. Then, right at the climax of the allied attack, the British fleet appeared. D'Estaing left the action at Newport and raced to meet his enemy at sea. A violent storm prevented the ensuing sea battle from being decisive, but Sullivan's men, left to face the English alone, were roughly handled ashore. When the French fleet put into Boston to refit, D'Estaing was amazed to discover that the Americans blamed him for the failure at Newport. There were anti-French demonstrations, and French blood was spilled. Washington was learning that an alliance is a mixed blessing, and that coalition warfare requires special methods.

Other than minor clashes, very little happened during the remainder of 1778. Then, as the year ended, the British seized Savannah, Georgia. It was a toehold in the South that they would keep and enlarge for some time.

A Quiet Year: 1779

Clinton was not strong enough to tackle Washington's Continentals in their mountain-protected redoubts above New York, while the Americans, without a fleet, were unable to launch an attack against the British in New York. It was a near-stalemate that pleased neither commander; each searched his meager resources and options in hopes of discovering some way to assume an offensive stance.

Clinton struck first. Late in May he suddenly seized the outposts at Stony Point and Verplanck's Point, cutting a major rebel east-west supply route and taking a position that threatened the Hudson Highlands. Washington at first feared for the safety of West Point, and maneuvered his army to protect that vital post. Then, when it grew clear that Clinton was content to remain at Stony Point, the Commander-in-Chief resolved to retake it. *(See Map 10.)*

"Mad" Anthony Wayne was selected to command the attack. While intelligence was painstakingly gathered and plans were carefully made, Steuben drilled handpicked troops on the West Point plain. When all was ready, Wayne advanced under stringent security measures on a moonless night, just before midnight on July 15. His plan called for a secondary attack against the enemy right, a demonstration against the center, and a main attack that would penetrate the British left. On pain of death, not a musket was to be loaded in the secondary or main attacks. Firing would be permitted, however, in the demonstration. Both the main

The Storming of Stony Point, July 1779

and secondary attacks were to be made in column. At the head of each was a forlorn hope* of 20 men led by a lieutenant; their task was to rush the barricades and physically force a small breach. Right behind them was an advance party of 150 soldiers, which would pour through the hole and widen the gap. Lastly came the main body, which would push on to destroy the garrison. Wayne led the main attack.

Just after midnight, contact was made by both columns. The British fired, but the forlorn hopes, ignoring the musketry, doggedly chopped through the wooden breastworks. At the sound of gunfire, the demonstration group charged down the center on the main road, shooting and shouting. It worked. Lieutenant Colonel Henry Johnson, commanding the garrison, counterattacked in the center with nearly half his defenders. They struck thin air. Before the disorganized British could recover and return to the defenses, Wayne's men had penetrated, sealing them out. A

*In earlier years, forlorn hope was a term used to describe a group of soldiers who had a difficult, often suicidal mission.

few redcoats continued to resist, and were bayoneted; most cried for quarter. At a price of 15 dead, Wayne had taken a post defended by more than 600 men.

In the overall context of the war, Stony Point was of negligible importance. As a matter of fact, Washington quickly destroyed the works and withdrew. But the splendid little affair was a great morale builder for the Patriots, and it served undeniable notice that the Continental Army was a professional army. Such an exploit would have been unthinkable to the rabble Washington had led in the first three or four years of the war.

Washington, establishing his headquarters at West Point, concentrated on strengthening the fortifications there while casting about for a location where he might gain yet another moral victory. Paulus Hook, located on the Hudson across from New York City, was isolated, vulnerable to a swift raid, and near enough to Clinton's headquarters to be embarrassing to the British should a raid succeed. Major Henry Lee, better known by his flamboyant sobriquet, "Light-Horse Harry," was entrusted with an attempt against it.

Although only 23 years old, Lee had proven himself to be a daring and capable cavalryman endowed with true fighting instincts—instincts that would be inherited by his son, Robert E. Lee. Lee's attack, on August 19, was not as wholly successful as Wayne's assault of Stony Point, but it further boosted American esprit and confidence.

Two other campaigns that had little immediate impact but were of far-reaching importance to the new nation were conducted in 1779. Weary of Indian depredations against the relatively unprotected frontier settlements, Washington decided to take advantage of the general lull in the war to strike back at the looters. He directed General John Sullivan to ravage totally the Iroquois lands in Pennsylvania and New York. Sullivan performed his mission well, and the Iroquois civilization never recovered from the blow. The menace was not entirely eliminated, however; the Indians surged back with renewed fury in succeeding years, but those were the spasmodic, futile blows of a dying cause.

George Rogers Clark, another leader in his twenties, had been sent in 1778 by the State of Virginia to oppose British and Indians in the present-day states of Kentucky, Illinois, Indiana, and Ohio. It was an ambitious project, especially considering the fact that his army numbered under 200 men! Climaxing a campaign that was astounding equally for results gained and rigors endured, Clark cornered and captured the British territorial commander at Vincennes in February 1779. He encouraged the fort's garrison to capitulate unconditionally by demonstrating what their fate would be otherwise—captured Indians were slain with hatchets by way of example beneath the stockade wall. Clark held the vast territory until war's end, thus insuring that the area would become a part of the United States. It would be hard—perhaps impossible—to find another example in history of so few accomplishing so much.

As the summer months passed, Washington chafed at the Allies' fading opportunity. D'Estaing had taken his fleet to the West Indies for the winter, but had indicated that he would return by June. New York could be taken and the British decisively drubbed, Washington felt, if D'Estaing would only appear. When the Frenchman did come he was three months late and several ports south, landing near the British base at Savannah in September. Upon learning of D'Estaing's arrival, Clinton evacuated Rhode Island and concentrated in New York; Washington's hopes of wintering in New York City went aglimmering. General Benjamin Lincoln marched down from Charleston to join forces with D'Estaing, but relations between the two were strained from the start. Both Frenchmen and Americans needed lessons on how to work within an alliance. In October, they launched an ill-advised and poorly executed assault on the entrenched British troops in Savannah. The repulse was bloody and deserved. D'Estaing sailed away once more, having accomplished nothing, and leaving Americans angrier than ever at their French allies.

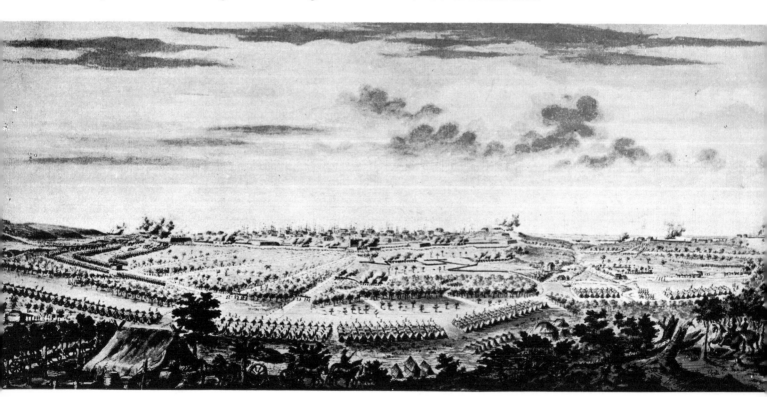

A French-American Force Tries Unsuccessfully to Recapture Savannah, October 1779

The Black Year: 1780

British superiority at sea, complete except during the rare forays of D'Estaing, provided Clinton with the advantage of interior lines. From his major base in New York he could move by ship to any spot on the American coast faster than Washington could march overland to intercept him. Encouraged by the allied defeat at Savannah, Clinton decided to make use of his fleet-endowed advantage to take Charleston, South Carolina. Ever since his failure there in 1776 he had wished for another try. Moreover, it seemed that success might be gained in the South, away from Washington and the stalemate in the North. As the new year rolled in, Clinton was aboard transports with a large, seasick invasion force.

After a terrible, six-week winter voyage, the expedition reached Savannah. There the troops were permitted a brief period of recuperation before landing near Charleston on February 11. At that point, Clinton inexplicably grew timid; he did not move for five weeks. Finally, on April Fools' Day, he laid siege to Charleston, which was defended by General Benjamin Lincoln and some 2,500 Continentals. Militia and armed townsmen swelled the number of defenders to approximately 5,000. *(See Map 11.)*

Charleston in 1780, like New York in 1776, was a trap. It, too, was defended for political reasons. But there the similarity ends. Clinton isolated the Patriot garrison and slowly, by regular approaches in formal siege operations, squeezed until Lincoln capitulated. On May 12, 1780, the United States suffered its greatest loss of the war when over 5,000 men became prisoners of the King. That same month, at Waxhaws, Lieutenant Colonel Banastre Tarleton—a dashing, 26-year-old English cavalryman, who would be remembered in history for his ruthlessness and for playing Varro* at the Battle of Cowpens—rode down and wiped out the last organized Patriot troops in the Deep South. The states of Georgia and South Carolina were once again under the Royal banner. Clinton departed for New York, leaving Cornwallis to command in the South. A violent, bitter war flared between British-supported Loyalists and Patriot partisan bands led by such men as Thomas ("Carolina Gamecock") Sumter, Francis ("Swamp Fox") Marion, and Andrew ("Wizard Owl") Pickens. It was often American against American. The guerrillas, while they could not recapture or even defend the southern states, forced Cornwallis to divert much of his already meager resources to securing lines of communication. The bloody, no-quarter nature of the clashes has prompted some historians to call

*Varro was the Roman consul who opposed Hannibal at the Battle of Cannae.

Francis Marion

Thomas Sumter

Andrew Pickens

Sumter, Marion, and Pickens Were the Most Prominent Southern Partisan Leaders During the Revolution

Banastre Tarleton

that period the first American Civil War.

Anxiously hoping to blunt the British in the South, Congress, without consulting the Commander-in-Chief, ordered southward General Horatio Gates, the hero of Saratoga. A body of Continentals under the command of Baron de Kalb had preceded him. Gates overtook them in North Carolina, and rushed into a premature campaign. Wiser officers counselled him to wait for supplies, but he arrogantly insisted that his army could live off the land. He started south only to learn that the area had already been picked clean by partisans. Such living as his troops managed was on green peaches and unripe corn. With a half-starved command, Gates met Cornwallis just north of Camden, South Carolina, on August 16. Intending to strengthen his soldiers with a full meal before battle, Gates ordered a hasty supper prepared, and issued molasses to wash it down. Not a better laxative has ever been discovered than half-cooked green corn and heavy black molasses; the Americans would find it difficult to remain in ranks during the ensuing fight. *(See Map 11.)*

Gates disposed his units in line and waited passively for the British to attack. If he had any plan at all, it has never been uncovered. His strength was about 4,000, of whom 1,000 were Continentals, but, astounding as it seems, he apparently thought he had 7,000! He himself took post 600 yards to the rear in the midst of a reserve of several hundred regulars.

Very little can be said of the battle itself. At the sight of British bayonets and the sound of the first shot or two, Virginia and North Carolina militiamen threw down loaded weapons and stampeded for the rear. Gates, caught up in the panic, spurred his horse north and, setting some kind of record for retreat, arrived at Charlotte 60 miles away on the same day. Meanwhile, the Continentals, unaware that they had been deserted by commander and comrades, fought on until they were destroyed. Horsemen were dispatched to run down the fugitive militia. The loss was so great that no accurate casualty lists were ever compiled. Perhaps as many as 1,000 Americans were killed, and by far the greatest number were Continentals. Another 1,000 were captured. In all, fewer than 800 survived the wild retreat. It was the bloodiest disaster to overtake the Patriots in the war; and it followed the heavy losses at Charleston by only two months.

Such a shocking loss could not have occurred at a worse time. American morale was at an all-time low. After five years of fighting, the nation was in a shambles. Paper money had so depreciated in value that it was practically worthless ($4,000 in paper might bring $1 in gold or silver); Congress was growing impotent and unable to supply its forces in the field (Washington had to beg the states for bread and meat). The Army had not been paid for months and was weary of living on half rations or less in a country rich in food; desertions were running about even with enlistments. In addition, France, whose entry into the war had raised such high hopes, had warned the United States that it must do more to help itself. France was reaching the limit of its financial ability to carry on the conflict. Set against that unpromising background, the military reverses of 1780 seemed to predict the death of the infant republic.

As Cornwallis moved undefeated into North Carolina, two events took place—one in New York and one in the hills of South Carolina—that stopped the string of British victories. On the Hudson, Benedict Arnold, by a stroke of fortune, was prevented from selling West Point to the enemy. In Tennessee, the "over the mountain" men decided to send an expedition against the invaders. The mountaineers met the English at King's Mountain, in South Carolina. Actually, it was American against American—irregulars all—except for an English officer commanding the Loyalists. Promptly annihilating their foe, the frontiersmen withdrew behind the Blue Ridge Mountains, well satisfied with their one foray of the war. Washington, too, was pleased by the unexpected aid. It gave him time to send reinforcements, including a shrewd general, southward.

"Over the Mountain" Men Rendezvous at Sycamore Flats Before the Battle at King's Mountain, October 1780

At King's Mountain, Loyalists are Overwhelmed by the "Over the Mountain" Men, 1780

General Nathanael Greene

Nathanael Greene Takes Command in the South

The general Washington entrusted with the Southern Theater was Nathanael Greene, a Quaker with non-pacifist notions, and an officer in whom the Commander-in-Chief had the utmost confidence. The choice was a good one.

Taking over from Gates in Charlotte, North Carolina at the end of 1780, Greene started with fewer than 1,000 Continentals. The ragged army lacked clothing and provisions, and had practically no systematic means of procuring them. Greene faced his problem realistically. Unlike Gates, he decided that he must not rush into battle against a superior British force. Instead, with the cooperation of Marion, Sumter, and Pickens, he would conduct essentially guerrilla operations, harrying Cornwallis' lines of supply and wearing down the strength of his army. Greene hoped for a gradual accretion of his own strength to the point where it would enable him to defeat a weakened British army in the field. As a first step, he had his engineers explore and map the surrounding country so that no move would have to be made without some knowledge of the terrain. Next he determined to get out of the devastated area around Charlotte and into richer country where he could live off the land. The best position was at Cheraw Hill in South Carolina, but because it was farther away than Charlotte was from Cornwallis' base at Winnsboro, to move there with his entire army would give the inhabitants the impression that he was retreating. *(See Map 12.)* He therefore decided to move only part of his army to Cheraw, sending the rest west under

Morgan, across the Catawba River into an area closer to Cornwallis' camp. This seeming violation of the principle of mass was amply justified in view of the type of operations Greene intended to conduct. Small, separate forces could live off the land much more easily than could one large force. Furthermore, it virtually forced Cornwallis to divide his army also, for the British commander soon perceived that if he moved against Morgan with his entire army, Greene could advance against Charleston, and that if he moved against Greene, Morgan could take the British posts in the west at Ninety-Six and Augusta.

Greene's plan was particularly effective in view of the character of the general opposing him. Unlike Clinton, Cornwallis was extremely—even rashly—aggressive, and was willing to cut loose from his supply depots on the coast 'to wage war in the interior. Disregarding Clinton's admonitions that he should push his designs against North Carolina only if it involved no risk to the British posts in South Carolina and Georgia, Cornwallis decided in 1781 to risk everthing on a successful invasion, practically burning his bridges behind him by depleting his Charleston base and bringing almost all supplies forward. Clinton's wisdom was greater than his forcefulness, and he allowed the headstrong Cornwallis to go his way. He was aware that his subordinate enjoyed greater support in London than he did, and that he had established separate channels of communication with the King's ministers. Divided command—not on paper in this case, but in practice—was once again to pave the road to British disaster.

Puzzled by Greene's dispositions, Cornwallis divided his army not into two but three parts. He sent a holding force to Camden to contain Greene, and directed Tarleton with a fast-moving contingent of 1,100 infantry and cavalry—a formation known as a legion—to find and crush Morgan. With his main army he moved cautiously up toward North Carolina, confidently expecting to cut off the remainder of Morgan's force after its defeat by Tarleton. On January 17, 1781, Tarleton finally caught up with Morgan near King's Mountain at a place called Cowpens. *(See Map 13.)* There Morgan had determined to make a stand, with his back parallel to the Broad River a few miles to his rear, and an open, sparsely forested area to his front and right. Morgan's force was numerically almost equal to that of Tarleton, but it was three-quarters militia, and his cavalry was greatly inferior.

Morgan fully understood the limitations of his militia, and adopted a plan whereby its capabilities could be used to full advantage. He selected a slight rise as the center of his position and formed his main line of Continental infantry on it, deliberately leaving his flanks open, ordinarily a dangerous thing to do. Well out to the front of the main line he posted Pickens' militia riflemen in two lines, instructing the first line to fire two volleys and then fall back to the second. The combined line was to fire until the British pressed them, and then fall back by a pre-arranged route to the rear of the Continentals and reform as a reserve. Behind the hill he placed Lieutenant Colonel William Washington's cavalry detachment, which was ready to charge the attacking enemy at the critical moment. Every man in the ranks was informed of the plan of battle and the part he was expected to play in it. Morgan walked from position to position, firing up his Continentals and calming down the militia. The men slept in their fighting formation so that they would be ready at dawn.

On finding Morgan ready for battle, Tarleton ordered an immediate attack. Moving forward in regular formation, Tarleton's men were checked by the militia fire. However, taking the retreat of the first two lines to be the beginning of a rout, the British troops then rushed headlong into the steady fire of the Continentals on the hill. A mistaken command caused the Americans to waver momentarily, encouraging the British still more. But Morgan steadied his line and stopped the redcoats' loosely controlled charge. At that juncture Washington's cavalry struck Tarleton's right flank, and Pickens' militia, having reformed, drove out from behind the hill to hit the British left. Snared in the jaws of a clever defensive-offensive maneuver, reminiscent of that used by Hannibal at Cannae, the British surrendered after suffering heavy losses. Tarleton managed to escape with only a small force of cavalry that he had held in reserve.

Cornwallis was still near at hand with the main British army, and Morgan had far too few men to risk another fight. He therefore swiftly marched to rejoin Greene, covering 100 miles and crossing two rivers in five days. *(See Map 12.)* Cornwallis moved much too slowly to trap him. With Greene's army again consolidated, Cornwallis was in about the same situation he had been in after King's Mountain. This time, however, he was too heavily committed to the campaign in North Carolina to withdraw. Hoping to match the mobility of the rapidly moving Americans, he destroyed all his superfluous supplies, baggage, and wagons. This action inspired Greene's next moves. Ignoring Morgan's advice to retreat west to the mountains, where Cornwallis could not follow, Greene determined instead to move north toward Virginia. In a nip-and-tuck chase, Greene reached the Dan River and safety just ahead of Cornwallis' hardmarching redcoats. It is important to note that Greene was highly pleased and Cornwallis quite unhappy at the outcome of the maneuvering, because at that moment there were no Continentals in the Carolinas or Georgia—on the map Cornwallis had conquered those three states; on paper,

he had won a victory. He had not destroyed the enemy army, however, and both generals appreciated the fact that the foe's fighting force—not real estate—is the decisive objective.

Discouraged, the British retired southward only to find the exasperating Quaker clinging to their heels. Reinforced, Greene thought the time ripe for a battle. Since four-fifths of his 4,300 soldiers were little more than recruits, he planned to fight a defensive battle patterned after Cowpens. Positioning his force at Guilford Court House, in North Carolina, he defied Cornwallis to come after him.

The long chase, the casualties, the sickness, the desertions, and the need to send out foraging parties had reduced Cornwallis' army to under 2,000, but all 2,000 were regulars. He did not hesitate to attack. On March 15, 1781, he assaulted Greene on Greene's ground. In the fiercely contested engagement, Cornwallis gradually got the upper hand. Greene, sensing the odds for victory fading, broke contact in late afternoon and moved off with his army intact. The British camped on the battlefield, but with a strength reduced by 30 percent. Although Greene had lost about the same number of men, his much larger force was proportionally less hurt. Cornwallis was no longer strong enough to remain in the field with Greene in the vicinity. Dejectedly he marched to the coast for reinforcements, and then headed for Virginia, where he would find a worse fate at a place called Yorktown.

Greene let Cornwallis leave and turned his attention to South Carolina and Georgia, where Lieutenant Colonel Francis Rawdon was defending 25,000 square miles with perhaps 8,000 men. Some 2,000 of those were at Camden, the site of Gates' rout, and the remainder were scattered among a myriad of small outposts. Greene, his army reduced to 1,500 Continentals by the departure of six-weeks militia, marched boldly towards Camden to fix Rawdon while he dispatched the legion of "Light-Horse Harry" Lee and the partisans of Pickens, Marion, and Sumter to capture the outposts one at a time.

On April 25, Greene and Rawdon fought the Battle of Hobkirk's Hill near Camden. The youthful Rawdon, then only 26, handed Greene, his senior by 13 years and several grades, a sound thrashing. Once more, though, the resilient Greene withdrew with an army intact, and once more the tactically victorious British were obliged to retreat.

Rawdon attempted to order all his remaining isolated garrisons to withdraw. Many did, but not all got the word. They were besieged, and most eventually fell to one of Greene's lieutenants. Greene himself laid siege to Ninety-Six, the most important British position in the interior after Rawdon gave up Camden. He spent four weeks in late May and June beating the garrison down, but just as he was on

The Battle of Guilford Court House, March 1781

the verge of victory, Rawdon broke through with a relief column, chased the Patriots off, and evacuated his men to Charleston.

Greene rested his worn troopers for several weeks and then took the field again, soon afterwards losing yet another battle at Eutaw Springs in early September. The British, however, were forced back into enclaves at Savannah and Charleston. Those two towns were evacuated the next year. Nathanael Greene, the general who could not win a battle, had brilliantly forced the enemy out of the southland in less than a year. As a strategist among the Patriots, he was second only to Washington; some would place him first.

The End: Yorktown

Strangely enough, Washington was reluctant to fight the battle that ended the war. From the time he was so ig-

nominiously ejected from New York, the Commander-in-Chief had harbored a deep-seated desire to recapture that port and redeem his defeat. In the summer of 1780, when a large French army under General Jean Comte de Rochambeau landed in Newport, Rhode Island, and the cooperation of a French fleet was promised in a final, all-out effort set for 1781, Washington saw his opportunity. At long last he would have the capability of striking at Clinton in New York.

Early in July, Rochambeau and Washington massed their two armies on the Hudson and began probing for weak spots in the English defense. No precise plan of attack was developed, for they were awaiting word of the fleet's arrival. This year the fleet would be commanded by Admiral Francois Comte de Grasse rather than the detested D'Estaing, a fact that was encouraging to the Americans. Also, the alliance was at last realizing its potential combined power, because Washington and Rochambeau enjoyed cordial relations and shared a mutual respect. Hopeful and eager, the

Comte de Rochambeau

two generals kept their armies poised for the blow that might end the long war as soon as the fleet arrived.

Then a thunderbolt struck. De Grasse sent a message saying that he would go only to the Chesapeake with his large fleet and some 3,000 troops. Worse, he would not remain past the start of the hurricane season in October.

Washington found himself in a predicament. He could not afford to ignore an opportunity to cooperate with a fleet after so many years, but a journey to Virginia would be risky. Half his Continentals would have to remain near the Hudson to protect it and to insure that British reinforcements remained in New York; his remaining forces and the entire French army would be required to march several hundred miles to rendezvous with the fleet and other Continentals in Virginia. Past performances of French admirals were not encouraging.

Nevertheless, with commendable decisiveness, Washington ordered a concentration in Virginia. Within a week, preparations were made, and the allied army began crossing the Hudson at Stony Point. A feint at Staten Island sufficed to keep Clinton in the dark as to their intentions until the troops reached Philadelphia. By then it was too late for Clinton to act. *(See Map 14.)*

The victory at Yorktown was made possible at sea. De Grasse eluded a pursuing British fleet to land his troops in Virginia, where they joined Americans under the command of Lafayette. From Newport, the Comte de Barras St. Laurent set sail with siege artillery and supplies. Hearing that, the British fleet sailed from New York in hopes of in-

tercepting him. On September 5, De Grasse sortied to engage the British Navy in the Battle of the Capes. While the two sea forces were inconclusively pounding one another, De Barras slipped into the Chesapeake, sealing Cornwallis' fate. The British vessels limped back to New York as the allies continued to draw the ring tighter around Yorktown. It would be just a matter of time. By September 26, the concentration was complete. French and American armies hemmed Cornwallis in on the land, while a French fleet blocked his escape by water. Formal siege approaches were opened on October 6.

Two aspects of the battle deserve special mention: the campaign was waged successfully by a coalition, and the Continental Army was professionally the equal of either of the two European armies. Washington was accepted as the overall commander of the combined French and American wings. The two national elements shared the work, dangers, and glory of the victory; and the French fleet made it possible. The rapid and effective progress of the siege works alone attests to the military prowess of the Continental units. Basically an engineering task, it would have been totally beyond the ability of most American officers in 1775.

After three days, allied cannon were moved up within range, and the artillery began a continuous pounding of the British defenses. Engineers opened a parallel,* and the guns crept closer. Two key redoubts were stormed and taken on the fourteenth. A second parallel was opened. On the night of October 16, Cornwallis attempted to escape to Gloucester, but a storm and a shortage of boats thwarted him. On the seventeenth, in a celebration of the fourth anniversary of Burgoyne's surrender at Saratoga, American and French guns delivered the heaviest cannonade yet. That night the British asked for surrender terms. When they marched out as prisoners on October 20, 1781, almost 10,000 men were lost to the services of the King. Allied casualties were about 300. For England, the Revolution in America was over for all practical purposes.

The long travail of the Patriots had led to ultimate success. Independence had been won on the battlefield. But it had never been a sure thing; often a slender thread had separated defeat from victory. America's victory—and England's defeat—sprang from many causes. The leadership of Washington would have to stand at the head of the list—try to imagine the war without him. British blunders played their part, too. Not that the inexperienced Americans committed fewer; theirs were just not as irredeemable. The

---

*In formal sieges, the assaulting forces advanced on the enemy works by digging trenches, or approaches, leading toward the enemy positions. Periodically, trenches generally perpendicular to the approaches were dug and called parallels. Artillery and infantry occupied the parallels, each one closer to the enemy line.

George Washington, Marquis de Lafayette, and Aide Tench Tilghman at Yorktown, 1781

difficulty of employing eighteenth century European tactics in eighteenth century America worked more to the detriment of English and Hessian units than to that of their more flexible foes. And, of course, French aid, advice, and manpower made it all possible. Finally, one would be remiss not to mention several smiles bestowed upon the Patriots by Lady Luck.

While this account has dwelt solely on operations in North America, there was also fighting in other theaters. As a rule, such clashes did not involve Americans, but the results had a great bearing on the outcome of the War of Independence. Battles outside of North America siphoned off English men, money, and ships that could otherwise have been massed against the Continentals. Gibraltar, India, the West Indies, and Central America provided the settings for most of the battles. John Paul Jones and other raiders carried the war against British shipping, even to the very shores of England. Although North America was the major and probably the decisive theater, the American Revolutionary War was definitely a worldwide war.

The Final Years

After Yorktown, the major fighting between England and America was finished. Then the waiting commenced. Washington took most of his army back to the Hudson Highlands and remained there for two more years. In some ways, those two years were more fraught with danger than any of the previous six. The war had not entirely ended, and the goals for which the Patriots had sacrificed so much for so long had not yet been attained. Skirmishes continued, but both sides avoided major actions while they waited for the signing of the expected treaty. During this time, the future of the United States depended in no small measure upon the activities of the Continental Army. Washington's task was to bring Patriot military power to bear in such a manner as to maintain and, if possible, strengthen American bargain-

ing power. Having won their war, Patriots had to win their peace.

Euphoria flooded the countryside following the capture of Cornwallis. Although the war had by no means ended, the major scenes of confrontation shifted away from the United States. The opening of negotiations in Paris added to the widespread sense of security by raising heady expectations of imminent peace. Relaxation was the natural reaction. After all, the bitter struggle had been interminably drawn out. Soldiers wanted to go home. State political leaders hoped to turn their attention to long-neglected local problems. The citizenry was manifestly tired of the prolonged conflict, and hungered for normality. Pressures for the dissolution of the nation's military establishment were all but irresistible. It took every bit of Washington's power and influence just to keep his army intact during the extended peace talks. What English generals had never been able to do—destroy the Continental Army—Americans very nearly let happen by default. It was true, as nearly everyone sensed, that the conflict had turned a decisive corner. Great Britain could probably not have won the American war in the years after Yorktown, because the King's external foes were too numerous and his internal opposition too powerful. Some students of the war contend that George Washington's greatest achievement was holding everything together during that final trying period. They may be right.

Complicated by the international scope of the war, peace negotiations dragged on interminably, but they were finally concluded with the outcome satisfactory to the Patriots. At last, the Commander-in-Chief's military task was finished. After an emotional farewell party with his officers in Fraunces' Tavern in New York City, Washington rode for Philadelphia to resign his commission. The path to ultimate victory had been long and rocky, but the tall Virginian had persevered. He had indeed been "first in war." Perhaps in that moment of triumph he recalled what he had told his men long ago in the early days of the struggle: "Every officer and soldier must act with fidelity and courage knowing that now the peace and safety of his Country depends (under God) solely on the success of our arms."

A Necessary Evil   3

The major problem associated with American military structure and policy, from the time of Cornwallis' surrender at Yorktown in 1781 to that December Sunday in 1941 when the Japanese struck Pearl Harbor, was the relationship of the militia to the standing army in the American force structure and national strategy. The obvious strategic advantages bestowed upon the young United States by accidents of geography and past policy, which resulted in the nation having its ramparts protected by ocean barriers to the east and south and by a vast and difficult expanse of territory to the north and west, meant that a navy designed essentially for coastal defense would be the nation's first line of protection against foreign invasion. Since the Navy traditionally was not seen as a serious threat to individual liberty or the political freedom of the nation, debates over its structure tended to revolve less around the fact of its existence than around questions of foreseeable foreign threats, expense, and technologies. This fact of life tended to insure that emotions, domestic politics, and confusion about roles and missions would focus to a greater degree on the structure of the land forces.

In 1783, Americans carried in their intellectual and political baggage a recently reinforced fear of standing armies and a natural trust in the *ideal* of relying upon the militia for defense against enemies, whether foreign or domestic. These beliefs were deeply rooted in historical interpretations and personal experiences. For more than a generation after the end of the Revolutionary War, lawmakers would rely upon this collective colonial and revolutionary experience when considering questions of United States military policy. At the same time, however, there were men—such as George Washington—who recognized that the new nation had a need for some type of standing army. For them, the major questions were how large an army was needed and could be afforded, and what missions should be assigned to it. In the first three decades of the new

nation's existence, Americans began to seek answers to those questions.

Heritage of Fear— Heritage of Courage

The legacy of Oliver Cromwell's New Model Army and the raping, pillaging hordes of the Thirty Years' War were memories as recent and vivid for those who labored for a better existence in North America as they were for those rulers and leaders who stayed behind and sought to limit the expense and isolate the greater proportion of the civil populace from the ravages of war on the continent of Europe. Along with the undeniable fact that among those who migrated to the colonies of England, France, and the Netherlands there were men who sought to escape the press gangs of contemporary European armies, however, we must also consider the equally undeniable truth that the colonies "were planted in an extraordinarily violent and ideologically polarized period of Western history."[1]

Those who came to colonize the New World used violence to achieve their ends if it appeared necessary. Indeed, those New World settlers and their opponents, be they Indian or European, seemed to favor total solutions to their disputes through the elimination of their enemies—witness the many massacres of Indian and white settlements throughout the western hemisphere by one antagonist or the other. Thus, while the older European states were moving into a period of warfare on the Continent that limited or mitigated the worst excesses of the wars of the recent past, the New World colonists were about to re-enact on a smaller scale horrors equal to those of the worst of Europe.[2]

European wars of the late seventeenth and eighteenth centuries may have been limited in scope and methods on the

European mainland, but as the table below shows, they were not limited in frequency or limited only to Europe.

European War	American Name
War of the League of Augsburg	King William's War, 1689–1697
The War of Spanish Succession	Queen Anne's War, 1702–1713
War of Jenkin's Ear	War of Jenkin's Ear, 1739
War of Austrian Succession	King George's War, 1743–1748
Seven Years' War	The French and Indian War, 1755–1763
American Revolutionary War, 1775–1783	American Revolutionary War, 1775–1783
Napoleonic Wars	Affected the United States in the Quasi-War with France and the War of 1812

European Wars of the Seventeenth and Eighteenth Centuries

Englishmen, to whom Americans owe their martial heritage, were aware that they were colonizing areas in the face of conflicting Indian, Dutch, Spanish, and French claims. Moreover, the unsettled state of the longstanding disputes between England and France especially affected the military situations in the colonies. First, it meant that the small standing forces sanctioned by Parliament during the periods of relative peace had to be reserved for the defense of the home islands. Second, in an era of slow and uncertain communications, it meant that there was always a danger of colonists being caught unaware by a sudden sweep of an enemy fleet or by a surprise Indian attack. Third, it meant that colonists might be isolated from each other and from England for extended periods as a result of war at sea or in Europe. Colonial charters and the realities of the frontier situation, therefore, dictated that, at a minimum, the colonists would have to be responsible for their own defense and be prepared to beat off attacks from the land and sea. Accordingly, it is no accident that the colonists were organized from the beginning to accomplish this mission, and it is understandable that Captain Miles Standish, Captain John Smith, and other professional soldiers accompanied them as military consultants. The primary reason for establishing the settlements was not military, and most colonists were not soldiers; but the old English militia tradition, dating back to the Assize of Arms of 1181, did serve as a model for those who braved the hazards of an ocean voyage and an unknown and possibly hostile shore.[3]

During the seventeenth century, the English colonists brought to America not only their precious basic legal and political rights as Englishmen,[4] but also an equally essential concept for survival in the New World—the militia obliga-

tion of military service. Unpopular as the militia obligation may have been in the contemporary English experience, in the forbidding and potentially hostile American environment, all able-bodied men between 16 and 60 years of age, with few exceptions, were expected to belong to a militia unit and to serve when called.[5]

As the frontier receded into the interior and the Indians became less of a danger in many areas, the militia might have fallen into complete disarray on the seaboard had it not been for the emergence of a new threat to keep its spirit alive. Beginning in about 1689, the English and the French were engaged in more or less continuous warfare that spilled over into the New World. Although the threat had always been real, previous periods of Anglo-French warfare had not affected the colonies. For example, when a French-Canadian force had moved into Iroquois country in 1666 to punish the Mohawks and had thus trespassed into New York territory, New York diplomatically ignored the incursion and did not retaliate, even though England and France were at war at the time.[6] After 1689, however, Anglo-French wars extended into the colonies. The colonists, with little or no help from the mother countries, were expected to wage war on their rival's colonies. Conditioned by the brutality of war with the Indians, perhaps angered by the French use of Indian allies, and bewildered by the way events 3,000 miles away in Europe could affect them so profoundly, the English colonists began to favor a strategy of annihilation. They clamored for nothing less than the total elimination of their enemies from the North American continent. While accomplishing this goal, which they did by 1763, they were forced to rely heavily on their own devices for military defense and success. Moreover, contact with the British regulars during the colonial wars usually resulted in serious friction between the colonists and the British troops. Disputes arose over questions of rank, methods of warfare, relative fighting abilities, and who should bear the expenses of wars in America.[7]

In these early English wars with the French, Spanish, and Indians, the colonial militia served as a defensive force, a training base, or a recruiting ground for the units that were used to fight these enemies. Since all able-bodied men theoretically belonged to the militia, an entire militia unit could be assembled only for a very short time, or else the home defense and the production of supplies necessary for the home front and the field units would suffer. The practice, therefore, was to seek volunteers from or to designate only a portion of the militia, in rotation, for extended service.

With the nearly complete English victory over the French in 1763, the threat to the English colonists from Canada was eliminated. The Spanish colonies were far away, and by then Spain was perceived only as a feeble threat to the populous English colonies in the New World. The colonists expected, therefore, to be done with military problems, and to be able to turn their full attention to civilian tasks. The British, although feeling the pinch of the debt from the Seven Years' War, were nevertheless determined to maintain a larger standing army overseas. English tradition and law would not allow a large standing force to be maintained in the home islands. The Government's decision was to keep a standing army in the colonies—and to tax the colonists for the upkeep of that force. The colonists deeply resented this action and viewed it as a violation of their basic rights as Englishmen; it was a key issue in the American Revolution. What is important to realize about England's decision is that the colonists, who had been used to looking after their own defense with citizen soldiers, were now burdened with the yoke of a standing army—one that all too soon did try to subjugate the colonists, both financially and politically.

The ringing indictments against the British monarch included in the Declaration of Independence reveal that the colonists did indeed fear oppression at the hands of the British Army:

> He has kept among us, in times of peace, Standing Armies without the Consent of our legislatures.
>
> He has affected to render the Military independent of and superior to the Civil Power.
>
> He has combined with others to subject us to a jurisdiction foreign to our constitution, and unacknowledged by our laws; giving his Assent to their Acts of pretended Legislation: For Quartering large bodies of armed troops among us: For protecting them, by a mock Trial, from Punishment for any Murders which they should commit on the Inhabitants of these states . . .
>
> He has abdicated Government here, by declaring us out of his Protection, and waging War against us.
>
> He has plundered our seas, ravaged our Coasts, burnt our towns, and destroyed the lives of our people.
>
> He is at this time transporting large Armies of foreign Mercenaries to compleat the works of death, desolation and tyranny, already begun with circumstances of Cruelty and perfidy scarcely paralleled in the most barbarous ages, and totally unworthy the Head of a civilized nation.

If British troops in America reinforced the American's long held fear of any standing army as one of the principal dangers to the liberty of a free people, the colonial wars' legacy of reliance upon the militia for defense was strongly reinforced and supported by the record of the militia during the Revolutionary War. In spite of disparaging remarks made about the militia by some Continental officers and expressions of frustration with real militia shortcomings by George Washington, the militia did make a valuable contribution. The cold realities of the military balance sheet throughout the war showed that the Continentals could not fight a major battle without significant reinforcements from the militia. If the semi-regular Continentals were better trained and steadier under fire, the militia were always more numerous and quite capable of giving a creditable performance when ably led or when allowed to fight in a manner that was consistent with their meager training and loose discipline.

The minutemen who opposed Gage's march to Lexington and Concord in 1775 were a part of the colonial militia. Burgoyne, marching south out of Canada in 1777, seems to have drowned in an ever deepening sea of militia. Burgoyne's German mercenaries were destroyed near Bennington, Vermont by a scratch force of hastily assembled militia, an ominous prelude to the fights around Saratoga where a mass of militia supported a precious leaven of Continentals in forcing the British to surrender. An aggregation of militia units from west of the Appalachian Mountains, made up of men who called themselves the "over the mountain" men, sallied forth for their one appearance of the war to soundly thrash a large body of Tories under the command of Major Patrick Fergusson at King's Mountain in 1780. Daniel Morgan made effective and imaginative use of his militia contingent's strengths and weaknesses in handing Banastare Tarleton's veterans a sound drubbing at Cowpens in 1781. Lord Cornwallis won the major battles but lost the campaign in the Carolinas in 1781 when he was taught an expensive lesson on attrition in warfare by the harassing tactics of militia groups operating under Greene's nominal direction. From Long Island, New York to Bucks County, Pennsylvania, from Maine's Penobscot to Georgia's pine barrens, the militia fought countless engagements with British regulars and Tory militia.[8] When the war ended, the most common military experience for citizens of the new nation was not service as a Continental, but service in local military units. The proud Patriots of 1783 may be forgiven for feeling that they had won the war with the militia.

In addition, militiamen made what was perhaps their most important contribution to Patriot success in the political battle for the loyalties of their fellow Americans. Militia units were used to enforce compliance with the Patriot political cause, and became the ultimate sanction of political authority within those districts not physically occupied by redcoats. Service in a militia unit, even if under coercion and duress, was seen as a test of political loyalty and a form of insurance against the depredations of one's neighbors. The militia unit, in sum, functioned as a politicizing agent.

The mutiny of the Pennsylvania Line in 1781 and the aborted Newburgh Conspiracy of 1783, among other incidents, further strengthened America's fear of standing armies as the Revolutionary War drew to a close. By 1783, the Americans had an inherited and recently reinforced fear of a standing army. Beyond that, the bankrupt condition of the nation's Treasury meant that the militia, whatever may be said of it, was the only army the United States could afford under the Articles of Confederation.

Arms and the Constitution

Money and military matters were problems of continuing concern to the Continental Congress throughout its existence. In 1783, the chronic lack of funds and consideration of a proper military establishment for peacetime were important and related political problems before the Congress. During the war, Congress had resorted freely to the printing presses for money, and relied on the states for troops. As the peace negotiations progressed, postwar problems began to claim more attention in Congress. Nationalist politicians, such as Alexander Hamilton and Superintendent of Finance Robert Morris, continued to press for a national source of revenue as opposed to continued requisitions on the states. The money raised by such a revenue measure would be used, among other things, to pay off the war debt, including the arrears in pay due to members of the Continental Army. Paying off these debts would secure the credit of the Government and consolidate its power to prevent disunion. A permanent regular federal source of income would also allow the Government to support a small military force that would awe the Indians and maintain the national prestige. Any national revenue source, however, would greatly strengthen the power of the central government over the states—a fact not lost sight of by the opposition.[9]

With the victory at Yorktown and the approach of peace, the urgency for united action by all the states was considerably diminished. Relieved from suffering under the power of a distant British government, the states were understandably reluctant to allow their own distant federal government equal powers. Under the Articles of Confederation adopted in 1781, there was no executive force. Congress had the responsibility for making decisions about many of the common problems of the states, but it had no power to implement its plans. There were no courts under the Articles to enforce the orders of the Government on either states or individuals. Without the power to tax, Congress even had to rely on essentially unenforceable requisitions on the several states for funds to pay its own expenses.

Enamored with their own power and intoxicated with the stunning success of the Revolution, the states became increasingly petulant in their dealings with Congress. Resolutions were ignored, requisitions for funds went unfilled, and states were dilatory even in sending representatives to Congress.

Nationalists in Congress, having failed once in 1781, tried again in 1783 to secure the necessary income for the Federal Government by amending the Articles to allow the Government to levy a 5 percent tariff on imports. Unanimous approval of all the states was required for such a measure. Both times the issue was raised, at least one state withheld its approval altogether, while others attached such restrictive conditions that the power to tax imports would have been practically meaningless.

The threats of military intervention that accompanied deliberations on the Impost of 1783 did not help either the revenue measure or the standing of the Continental Army in the eyes of the states. The veiled threat of an officers' revolt represented by the Newburgh Addresses, which only the astute personal intervention of Washington squashed, and the mutiny of the Philadelphia barracks, which frightened Congress right out of that city and into New Jersey, seemed to signify to many the evils that could be expected from a standing army.

In the aftermath of the Newburgh Conspiracy, which collapsed in March 1783, Congress took up the question of peacetime military problems. On April 4, Congress appointed a committee, chaired by Alexander Hamilton and dominated by nationalists, "to provide a system for foreign affairs, for Indian affairs, [and] for military and naval establishment."[10] Hamilton immediately wrote to the nation's foremost military authority, George Washington, asking for recommendations regarding a permanent military policy for the United States. Washington, after consulting his generals and Governor George Clinton of New York, replied from Newburgh on May 2, 1783 with his "Sentiments on a Peace Establishment."

Washington's response is important, because it represents not only his thoughts on the military establishment, but also the consensus of informed military men of the day.[11] The advice Washington received from his consultants, and that which he gave to the congressional committee, was remarkably uniform in assessing the military needs of the nation. To Brigadier General John McAuley Palmer, who rediscovered these long forgotten "Sentiments" nearly a century and a half later, this uniformity of opinion indicated that the question of a proper peacetime military establishment "had been the subject of thoughtful study and fre-

George Washington and His Generals

quent discussion at Washington's headquarters."[12]

Washington and his advisors unanimously recommended a standing army. "A regular and standing force," wrote Washington, "for Garrisoning West Point & such other Posts upon our Northern, Western, and Southern Frontiers, as shall be deemed necessary to awe the Indians, protect our Trade, prevent the encroachment of our Neighbors of Canada and the Floridas, and guard us at least from surprizes; Also for the security of our Magazines." Admittedly "a large standing Army" was a threat to the liberties of the country, "yet a few troops," under the circumstances, were, "not only safe, but indispensably necessary" in Washington's view. The general thought that a regular force of 2,631 officers and men would be sufficient for the country's peace establishment. The Continental Army would be paid and disbanded under his scheme, and the new peace establishment would then be "considered as a change in, if not the commencement of our Military System." Only those Continentals who had enlisted for three years would be retained to form the basis of the new army.[13]

After discussing the organizational structure of the regular force, the reasons behind its deployment into specific posts around the country, and other details of command, logistics, and administration, Washington addressed the other major aspect of his proposed peacetime military establishment, the militia. There it was—the melding of the militia tradition with the standing army.

Economic necessity, strategic setting, and political reality all were considered by the Commander-in-Chief as he developed the concept of the small regular force he proposed. He recognized the happy strategic situation the nation enjoyed as a result of its "*distance* from the European States . . . their numerous regular forces and the Insults and dangers which are to be dreaded from their Ambition." He also took into account the Confederation's thin financial resources, which limited the size of the regular forces to a number less than adequate for the nation's defense. Equally important politically was his realization that even if the country were "more populous & rich," it still could not maintain a standing army adequate for the job "without great oppression of the people."

Longstanding tradition provided the obvious solution to this dilemma. National militia, placed on a respectable footing, would provide the "great Bulwark of our Liberties and independence." Deficiencies in funds and trained regulars would be offset once again by the numbers the militia would provide. Men of Washington's persuasion felt that, "every Citizen who enjoys the protection of a free Government, owes not only a proportion of his property, but even of his personal services to the defence of it." The concept of universal military obligation was retained in the proposal that every able-bodied male citizen from 18 to 50 years of age be enrolled in the militia. To make that militia respectable in the eyes of the nation's allies as well as its potential enemies, the war leaders thought that the militia ought to be uniformly organized and drilled under federal supervision. If the militia were well regulated, they added, it would be a sufficient basis for an effective national defense system.

Washington's plan for the peace establishment also included establishing arsenals and "manufactories" for the required military stores. In addition to "Military Manufactories and Elaboratories," he proposed the establishment of military academies "to keep alive and diffuse the knowledge of the Military Art"—a worthy goal.

After digesting Washington's "Sentiments" and other opinions presented to the committee, Hamilton presented the committee's own plan to the Congress on June 17. It was an inauspicious time, because four days later tipsy recruits of the Pennsylvania Line* surrounded the Congress and demanded their pay. This mutiny forced the Congress to move to Princeton, New Jersey, where it continued to wrangle over other issues long repressed by the war. Dissension over money and related military issues was so intense that not even a personal visit by Washington to Princeton in August could convince the Congress of 1783 to consider the question of the peacetime military establishment until late October. Then, the lawmakers rejected the Hamilton Committee's revised proposals.

Plagued from the start by economic considerations and legal questions of Congress's authority to even raise and support a national peacetime military establishment, the question of a standing army was put aside as Congress became enmeshed in the politics of western land claims by the various states. At the last possible moment of the 1784 session, Congress finally acted by discharging all that remained of the Continental Army but for 80 artillerymen who were retained to guard the military stores at West Point and Fort Pitt. Having disbanded the Continentals, Congress called for the immediate recruitment of eight infantry and two artillery companies of militia volunteers. In all, 700 men were to be raised for one year from Connecticut, New York, New Jersey, and Pennsylvania. This small force of men was the beginning of the Regular Army of the United States.[14]

Military Weakness and National Humiliation Force Action

Congress envisioned the 700 militiamen it called forth as having a twofold mission. Slightly more than half of them were to occupy those forts held by the British to insure "protection of the northwestern frontiers," while 300 of them were to provide protection for American commissioners negotiating with the Indians.[15] It quickly became apparent that this small standing army was completely inadequate for the assigned tasks. The British, the Indians, and

even fellow citizens of the troops made this point patently clear.

Under the terms of the final treaties signed at Paris in early September 1783, the British were to evacuate a number of posts they held in the Northwest Territory of the United States. *(See Map 15a.)* Canadian fur traders and the settlers in upper Canada protested this provision of the treaty so effectively that while the King officially commanded his subjects to comply with the treaty, his ministers and the Governor General of Canada received secret orders to retain the disputed posts. The British excused their retention of the garrisons on United States soil by charging that the Americans had violated the treaty of peace. With the Continental Army reduced to a very small remnant of 80 men and the new regiment just being raised, the United States was in no position to force the British to comply.[16]

The weakness of the Federal Government prevented Congress from enforcing that section of the treaty which required that neither side pass laws impeding collection of private debts contracted before the war. When some states passed laws obstructing the British collection of prewar debts, Congress was helpless to prevent such a blatant violation of the treaty terms. The failure of the states to follow the recommendation of Congress required by the treaty for restoration of confiscated Loyalist property further weakened the case of the United States for withdrawal of the British garrisons. In vain, John Adams, the American Minister to England, protested the British refusal to evacuate. The English ministers, however, knew that there were no troops to back up the American protest.[17]

African pirates and the Spanish also took advantage of American military and naval weaknesses in the 1780s. The predictable result was further national humiliation.[18]

The tiny Army neither inspired fear in the Indians nor effectively kept squatters off either Indian or speculators' lands. Treaties with the Indians could not keep pace with the vigorous thrust of western settlement that followed the war. Land grants to Continental soldiers and the lure of unoccupied lands led many pioneers westward. *(See Map 15b.)* Encouraged by British arms and British presence in the Northwest Territory, the Indians fought to resist white incursion. The Army was equally powerless to protect the treaty rights of the Indians or to prevent squatters from occupying public or private lands. Neither could the Army, cooped up in its ever increasing string of forts, protect the squatters and legitimate pioneers from the Indians' retaliatory measures. Over 1,500 settlers were either killed or captured by Indians in Kentucky territory alone during the Confederation period.[19]

While Lieutenant Colonel Josiah Harmar's First American Regiment was being thinly dispersed over the

---

*During the American Revolutionary War, state military organizations were called "lines," although the term more correctly denoted the infantry elements that made up the "line" of battle of an army.

Brevet Brigadier General Josiah Harmar

Northwest Territory in a vain attempt to control the Indians and maintain some sort of order among land-hungry settlers, events were occurring that more dramatically demonstrated the perils of an impotent central government.[20] During the summer and winter of 1786, the specter of rebellion again stalked the land—first in New Hampshire, where 200 armed men invaded the legislature's chambers at Exeter and demanded cancellation of all debts and paper money, and then in Massachusetts, where wider rebellion raged.

Oppressed equally by heavy debts, heavy taxes, a scarcity of hard currency, barren lands, postwar depression, and an indifferent state government, the inhabitants of western counties of Massachussetts rebelled, paralyzing the courts and legal system with mob actions which put an end to the collection of debts and taxes. Fearful of being charged with treason for their disobedience, the disaffected elements organized a sufficiently strong force led by Daniel Shays to prevent the Supreme Court at Springfield from returning indictments against them. From the last week in September until the following March, the court dared not meet again in western Massachusetts.[21]

Keeping up such effective opposition to the state government required extensive organization. The insurgents organized into armed groups under a number of leaders, the most memorable of whom was Shays, ex-Continental captain and veteran of Bunker Hill, Saratoga, and Stony Point. Once organized, the armed bodies marched over the state seeking the redress of grievances, as well as arms, ammuni-

tion, and recruits. The national arsenal at Springfield, with its store of small arms, ammunition, and cannon, was among the points severely threatened by rebellious elements that last week in September and again in January 1787. The Federal Government, hampered by restrictions in the Articles of Confederation, was powerless to intervene, or even to protect the arsenal; it was ultimately saved by loyal militia, whose commander, Major General William Shepard, twice defied the Federal Government by arming his troops from the stores at the arsenal.[22]

Under cover of a real Indian threat on the western frontier, Congress authorized an increase in the strength of the Army to 2,040, but few of the additional forces could be raised. Massachusetts, fearful that national recruiting efforts would hamper her own attempts to suppress the uprising, forbade Continental recruits raised there to take the field. Once again the Confederation tasted the bitter fruit of national humiliation. Snubbed by state governments and unable to defend its own war stores, the Confederation was propelled at last by the shock of Shays' Rebellion to consider reform. Every state but Rhode Island agreed to send delegates to Philadelphia that spring to what was to become the Constitutional Convention of 1787.[23]

The Military Clauses of the Constitution

If military problems were not the only problems the delegates to that Philadelphia convention of 1787 came to consider, they were, however, important problems. The Constitution of the United States was designed to correct many of the ills under the Articles of Confederation. Not the least of these was the military impotence of the Federal Government, which had so recently led to national humiliation. The document that emerged from their deliberations was, as historian Walter Millis has written, "as much a military as a political and economic charter."[24]

The exact relationship of the militia and the standing army in the American force structure was not resolved by the Constitution. Both forces received due attention, but it is important to note that for the first time, Congress clearly had both the power "to lay and collect Taxes" and "to raise and support Armies." The idea that there might be a continuing requirement for a standing army had found a place in the basic law of the land. But the delegates were suspicious of a standing army's potential to run amuck or to fall prey to sinister influences. Even those who favored a standing army were concerned over the possibility that it might be used to support a wide spectrum of abuses of federal power. The solution, as was so often the case in the Constitution, was to distribute the powers and responsibilities into as many hands as was practicable, including the legislative and executive branches of the Federal Government, the state governments, and the people.[25]

It was a careful balance that the framers of the new document had to strike in order to provide for the common defense against foreign enemies and domestic insurrection, while also insuring domestic tranquility by not intruding too deeply into either the sovereignty of the states or the rights of the individual citizen. Besides taxing and keeping an army, Congress was given other military powers. It was entrusted with the power to "declare" war and issue letters of marque; to provide and maintain a navy; to make the rules and regulations for the land and naval forces; to "provide for calling forth the Militia to execute the Laws of the Union, suppress Insurrections and repel Invasion;" and to organize, arm, and discipline the militia of the states. These were very important powers to be entrusted to any single branch of the Federal Government. One check on the Congress, over half of whose members faced reelection every other year, was that no appropriation of money to be used for the Army was allowed for a longer term than two years. (No such limitation of funds was applied to the Navy.) Another check on Congress was the insertion of a clause designating the President the "Commander-in-Chief of the Army and Navy of the United States and of the Militia of the several states, when called into the actual service of the United States." Also, to the President went the power to "nominate . . . officers of the United States," but this was a shared power with the Congress, as the "advice and consent" of the Senate was required on his nominations.[26]

Warmaking power and all that went with it were reserved for the Federal Government by these provisions. However, there were checks on the federal powers, such as the two-year limitation on army appropriations which would·prevent Congress from making the standing army too onerous a burden on the people. By giving command of the federal forces to the President, the delegates insured against his leading a coup, since such a blow would be struck against the President himself. By giving Congress control of the funds, they further insured that the President would not use the Army against the Congress, imitating Cromwell's move against Parliament over a century earlier. But although the states were willing to give up some of their powers to a central government when protected in this way, they were not willing to surrender their military power totally. The dangers inherent in a system in which a federal government is supported by a standing army were perceived as being too great. Although the states were expressly prohibited by Section 10, Article I, of the Constitution from maintaining their own standing forces in times of peace, they were confirmed in their control of the militia. To them went the power to appoint militia officers and to exercise authority over militia training "according to the discipline prescribed by Congress." For the states and the people, the militia would be the check on the power of a standing army. It would also be the nation's chief reliance in wartime and the state's coercive force to maintain order.[27]

The rights of the people were protected against the power of the state and federal governments in several ways. First, the method of electing congressmen (but not senators) protected the public's interest in money matters—such as military appropriations—that originated in the House of Representatives. Second, since the people were the militia, it was inconceivable that they could be "brought into the field and made to commit suicide on themselves."[28] Third, such a hue and cry was raised over the lack of a Bill of Rights to the Constitution, that the first 10 amendments were passed and ratified so quickly that they may be considered to be a part of the original document for our purpose here. The second amendment, guaranteeing the right of the people to keep and bear arms, was "intended to secure the people against the mal-administration of the Government."[29] The third amendment prohibited the Government from billeting soldiers in the people's homes. This provision protected the people from the expense of providing for these unwonted and unwanted guests, and from the overt control over their activities that such soldiers could easily exercise. Finally, lest there be any doubt about the importance of the people to future governments, the ninth and tenth amendments specifically reserved to the people those rights and powers not specifically delegated to the United States or the respective states.

Both citizen-soldiers and professional soldiers were blessed by the Constitution. The power to raise and maintain a standing army was clearly present, but the relationship of that army with the militia was unresolved. Much of the controversy over ratification of the Constitution focused on the military clauses.[30]

Two competing policies for defining the relationship between the militia and the standing army emerged from the debates surrounding ratification. First, there was the preparedness doctrine favored by the Federalists in 1788, and by many others since. Rooted in nationalist political philosophy and Continental Army experience, this doctrine, which had already been articulated once in Washington's "Sentiments" and would be urged again before the First Congress by Secretary of War Henry Knox, emphasized the importance of the standing army *together* with a well trained, "well regulated" militia. The idea was to give the

Major General Henry Knox

nation a basic working military capacity in peacetime, and to centralize and professionalize defense planning and preparation. Hamilton and Knox, who advocated this view, saw a small standing army as a nucleus for a wartime regular army, as a model for the militia, and as an agency to facilitate orderly expansion in the West. As part of the standing forces package, the preparedness advocates of the 1780s and 1790s called for national military academies, stocks of supplies, and "manufactories" for producing arms, ammunition, and cannon. Principally, because a large standing army was neither financially nor politically feasible, they sought an improved national militia that would be a truly formidable force of trained citizen-soldiers under professional federal direction. Security from outside threats included internal order, national organization, and, of course, safety from internal rebellion.[31]

Antifederalists in the 1780s, and the later Republicans in the 1790s, slowly formulated a second theory, which entrusted the militia with the entire responsibility for national defense—to include a naval militia of "sea fencibles." A tiny force of Regulars was grudgingly admitted to garrison a few forts, such as West Point, and to maintain a meager stock of federal war reserve stores. But, proclaimed the Antifederalists, America, which was basically secure behind 3,000 miles of ocean and isolated at last from European rivalries, need not squander her resources or risk her liberties to the dubious care of a standing army raised for protec-

tion. The people, armed and organized militarily, were the only sure defense against either foreign or domestic enemies. A strong central government backed by the coercive power of a large standing army was more of a danger than were far-off British or Spanish armies. Any threat, even on the frontier, could be handled by a locally or regionally organized militia, which, as always before, could make up for what it lacked in training and discipline with sheer numbers. If a major war were to erupt with a European power, as it had in 1775, a wide and stormy Atlantic would provide adequate time to organize an appropriate national force. Domestic tranquility was of little concern to the Antifederalists, who saw any government that relied on the Army for its support as despotic and not worthy of continuing. Order would be maintained by the states' legal processes or the militia, which after all was the people.[32]

Neither position could gain uncontested supremacy or a clear national consensus. In the meantime, while sedate discussions of theory continued, violence began to overtake theory on the frontier.

The Militia Act of 1792

Henry Knox, perhaps taking a cue from the constitutional provision for the Congress "to provide for organizing, arming and disciplining, the Militia," presented his plan for the "arrangement of the militia of the United States" to President Washington and the second session of the First Congress in January of 1790. The plan was the latest iteration of the Federalist preparedness doctrine. (The old Continental Congress had seen similar plans before, starting with Washington's "Sentiments." In 1786, Knox had presented a plan to the Congress.) Even the slightly modified plan was still too ambitious for Congress. Although only a modest standing army of 2,033 officers and men was recommended, all men from 18 to 60 years of age were to be classified, organized, and rather rigorously trained in the skills of the soldier—and all this was to be done under federal supervision. Too much was required of the militia, and too much power was given to the Federal Government at the expense of the states. Congress was not pleased. Deliberation, not action, was the result.[33]

While Congress contemplated, trouble was brewing on the frontier. Encouraged by the continuing presence of the British in the Northwest and enraged by the continuing expansion of the white frontier, the Indians understandably became more and more belligerent. The settlers, in their turn, became more and more insistent that the Government adopt a more militant policy. To protect frontiersmen on lands legitimately purchased from the Federal Government, Congress increased the Army from 786 troops to 1,216 in April 1790. Governor Arthur St. Clair of the Northwest Territory and Brigadier General Josiah Harmar, despairing of the immediate prospects for peace, decided that a show of force was required.[34]

Harmar, reinforced by 1,000 Kentucky militiamen and 500 more from Pennsylvania, led the first major military expedition of the standing army of the United States to disaster. Neither the militia nor the Regulars earned much glory in that inept autumn campaign of 1790. The Indians were not intimidated; they were emboldened, encouraged, and infuriated.[35] *(See Map 15b.)*

With Indian harassment along the frontier increasing following Harmar's defeat, Congress voted for a reorganization of the Army and the enlistment of more troops in March 1791. The new law authorized a second infantry regiment to be added to the Army, and further authorized the President to call into service two additional regiments of temporary federal troops or whatever militia might be required for six months. Included in the reorganization was the authority for a major general to command the Army. Washington named Governor St. Clair to that office and directed him to command a new expedition against the Indians.[36]

Lassitude, delay, and peculation characterized this second attempt to impress the Indians with the young nation's military prowess. Major General St. Clair led a faltering,

Major General Arthur St. Clair

bickering, untrained, disorderly mass of men to a defeat even greater than Harmar's. On November 4, 1791, the Indians caught St. Clair's main body in a poorly sited encampment astride the Wabash River and skillfully butchered it.[37]

Goaded by the sting of the second military disaster in two years, Congress responded in March 1792 with a third reinforcement and reorganization of the Army. The March legislation increased the artillery battalion and two regiments of infantry already authorized to full strength. The Regulars were further reinforced by three regiments of infantry enlisted for three years or until peace was made with the Indians—whichever came first—and by the addition of four troops of light dragoons. Four brigadier generals were authorized to assist the major general commanding the Army, and some further administrative adjustments were made to improve the lot of the troops.[38] Negotiations with the Indians and the desire to insure success postponed for two years the use of these forces in active combat.

During the flurry of military interest occasioned by St. Clair's defeat on the Wabash, Congress also attended to its long languishing militia proposals. Secretary Knox's 1790 proposals had disappeared into the congressional committee routine to be replaced by a wholly new plan prepared by a House committee. During floor debates in February and March of 1792, the committee's bill was further weakened until it was able to pass the House by a vote of 31 to 27, and the Senate by the more substantial margin of 22 to 1. Finally in May, after two years of deliberation, "An Act more effectually to provide for the National Defense, by establishing an Uniform Militia throughout the United States" became law. In actuality, the Militia Act of 1792 did little to establish a truly uniform militia. It was more of a gesture than a directive. Nonetheless, it was important, for it was to remain the basic law of the land on the subject for 111 years. The act preserved and legalized under the Constitution the universal military obligation of the militia tradition. Every able-bodied white male citizen, age 18 to 45, was to be enrolled. Militiamen were required to furnish their own weapons and equipment within six months of their enrollment. Other provisions included an attempt to create the office of Adjutant General in each state. By the terms of the act, each state's Adjutant General was supposed to furnish an annual report on the condition of the state's militia to his governor and to the President. The act also went into details of organization in an attempt to standardize the various units, but attached to this portion of the bill was the emasculating phrase: "if the same be convenient." Because no penalties were prescribed for noncompliance, in the last analysis the act was more of a recommendation to the states than a law.[39]

As the basic foundation of citizen service, the Militia Act of 1792 has been roundly condemned and abused by regular army advocates, such as Emory Upton.* The avenues of attack were many: no federal standards of training and competence were provided; no standard arms were furnished, leaving weapons selection largely up to the whim of the individual militiaman; no federal means of enforcement were made available.[40] If military efficiency were the only goal of the act, the Uptonian school was probably right. But, at that point in America's growth, military efficiency was only one of many goals that had to be carefully weighed and balanced. More important to the young and still poor nation were the competing civilian goals, such as the exploitation of the country's still largely unexplored potential. If it did nothing else, the act preserved the nation's inherited tradition of the universal military obligation of its citizens. That achievement was valuable. To have expected more of an individualistic, scattered, agrarian society was to expect too much. The law, in retrospect, was appropriate, and if it was not always effective, at least it served until a substitute for the militia could be improvised.[41]

While the Militia Act of 1792 was one cornerstone of American military policy fashioned from the concern caused by St. Clair's defeat, another was the army that Major General Anthony Wayne fashioned from the 5,000 federal troops authorized by the 1792 legislation. Embarrassed by the two previous thrashings administered by the Indians, Washington's administration was determined not to suffer a third. With the failures of the former commanders' generalship duly noted and with an equal conviction that the military inefficiency of the militia was also at fault, the Washington administration sought a new combination for victory over the Indians. The first step was to obtain the authority to build an army capable of victory. For this, Washington and Knox were convinced that a sufficient force of regular troops was required. Congress agreed when it authorized five regiments to be raised, and further assisted the administration by authorizing four brigadier generals to complete the reorganization of the Army into the Legion of the United States. Steuben had earlier suggested the legionary structure to facilitate campaigning in the wilderness. The Army, or Legion as it was now called, was divided into four sub-legions, each of which was composed of about 1,200 men commanded by a brigadier. The sub-legions were similar to the divisions being employed at about the same time by the French Army. They were designed to enhance tactical flexibility by creating miniature armies complete with the artillery, cavalry, and infantry needed to operate independently in sustained combat.[42]

Washington and his Cabinet then gave careful consideration to who should command the Legion. Many names were put forward from the list of distinguished Revolutionary War generals. Regional politics and the military sensibilities of the generals all complicated the selection process. Finally, Washington reluctantly picked "Mad" Anthony Wayne, the brave, salty combat commander who had captured Stony Point in 1781 with a night bayonet assault. Wayne was the right man for the job. His politics were correct, and he was well known to Washington and Knox. He had the mind and the experience needed for a major independent command together with a dominating desire to meet and destroy the enemy. Events would prove the appointment to be one of the most brilliant of the Federalist era.[43]

Wayne understood the administration's need to gain political support for further military operations against the Indians. While the Government sought peace through diplomacy, Wayne recruited and rigorously trained a superb fighting force. He moved the main body of the army into the wilderness, far from the seamy distractions of Pittsburgh. There, through firm regulatory measures used on errant officers and enlisted soldiers alike, he established discipline in his force. Every officer was responsible for drill according to Steuben's *Blue Book*. Camp sanitation, health services, and proper supply economy all received attention from the entire chain of command. Marksmanship and the art of field fortification were also emphasized. Esprit de corps gradually grew under Wayne's expert nurturing.[44]

By the time peace negotiations with the Indians failed, Wayne had created a reliable fighting force. The onus for the hostilities had been shifted back to the Indians and their British mentors by public disclosure of the official British encouragement of the Indians and by Indian attacks on Fort Recovery, which the Legion had built on the site of St. Clair's defeat. Thus in the summer of 1794, 2,000 of Wayne's regulars, reinforced by 1,500 mounted Kentucky militia, headed north into hostile territory toward Fort Miami, a newly constructed stronghold that the haughty Britons had erected on United States soil. Finally, on August 20, within earshot of the British garrison, Wayne soundly defeated a force of Indians and Canadian militia in the Battle of Fallen Timbers. *(See Map 15b.)* This victory broke the Indian hold on the old Northwest Territory. Humiliated by Wayne's victory under their very noses and with their influence over the Indians now clearly in decline, the British received a decisive push toward the evacuation of their posts on United States soil. Wayne had done well in battle and had given the infant Army its first taste of excellence. Within 16 months of his victory, however, Wayne

---

*Emory Upton, a distinguished American Civil War combat leader and military intellectual, wrote at length on American military policy in the decades following the Civil War.

Major General Anthony Wayne at Fallen Timbers, August 1794

died of illness. He would be remembered by some as the Father of the Regular Army.[45]

Seacoast Fortifications and National Strategy

Wayne's victory at Fallen Timbers not only provided an amelioration of the Indian threat, but also was useful as a bargaining tool with the British. While Wayne was busy preparing to deal with the Indians on the western frontier, others were becoming increasingly concerned with what appeared to be an ever growing foreign threat to the eastern seaboard. A new, generation-long series of wars, all of which were associated with the French Revolution and Napoleon, at this time engulfed Europe and the world. England and France, at odds again, began to draw America, much to her surprise, into the whirlpool of wars centered in Europe. The Old World antagonists vied with one another

in inflicting insults on American honor at sea while at the same time attempting to woo, cajole, or coerce America into actively entering the conflict.[46]

The British angered the Americans by instituting an aggressive policy at sea. This policy, although aimed at Revolutionary France, threatened America's shipping and neutrality rights. When the Royal Navy began to harass French trade routes to the West Indies, France opened her Caribbean ports to American shipping in order to keep her colonies from starving. Sniffing profit, American ships by the hundreds made way for the tropical French ports. Great Britain's reaction was swift. Citing a policy she had enunciated in 1756, Orders in Council were issued authorizing the seizure of neutral cargoes bound for French ports. Hundreds of American ships were seized, and the American crews were callously jailed or, worse, impressed into the Royal Navy. American protests asserting the neutral doctrine that "free ships make free goods" were ineffective against the Royal Navy's contention that neutral nations could not in time of war open trade routes that were prohibited in peacetime. Since there was no navy to back the American doctrine, the British position prevailed.[47]

Because of the unbridled power demonstrated in 1793 by the fervent military forces loosed by the French Revolution and British actions at sea and in the Northwest during 1793 and 1794, the United States was forced to take a hard look at its total defense posture. Faced with potential enemies many times more powerful than the Indians, it was no surprise that the President and the Congress agreed that the current posture was inadequate. Early in 1794, Congress responded with the Naval Act of 1794, which marked the beginning of the United States Navy. Probably because the six-frigate navy authorized by the act was so miniscule compared to either the British or the French fleet, the act's preamble stated that it was designed to protect the nation's commerce from "the depredations committed by the Algerine corsairs."[48] The great amount of time the Third Congress devoted to commercial relations and the losses that United States shipping suffered at the hands of the British, however, strongly suggests another interpretation.

Other measures taken by the Third Congress support the alternate thesis that the Navy was also expected to protect our commerce and shores from other European depredations. Obviously, the "Algerine corsairs" were not going to venture from their Mediterranean lairs to attack the American seacoast. Neither the British nor the French, with their land forces engaged in Europe, were as likely to send invasion forces as some in 1794 may have believed, but either or both might have sent raiding forces sufficiently strong to demand heavy ransoms from ports and towns along the seacoast. The same congressional committee that had recommended the building of a six-frigate navy hurriedly studied the problem of defending the Atlantic seaboard. Five weeks after taking up the question, the committee recommended the fortification of 16 ports and harbors against surprise naval attack. The committee further recommended "that the several places, to be fortified, be garrisoned by troops in the pay of the United States." The Congress quickly considered the report, increased the number of ports to be protected to 21, and authorized the President to fortify the ports and to garrison them with "troops on the Military Establishment of the United States." Other legislation provided for the establishment of a Corps of Artillerists and Engineers, presumably to oversee the construction of the harbor defenses and to man the guns.[49]*

The year 1794 was a busy one for the military forces of the United States. While the Regulars were subduing the Indians at Fallen Timbers and preparing to build and man what has been called the First System of Seacoast Defenses, the militia were called upon to enforce the law and suppress insurrection. Western Pennsylvanian corn farmers did not think highly of the whiskey excises of 1791 and 1792—or of any other tax for that matter. Persistent opposition to the whiskey taxes in particular—whether principally by the sellers or the drinkers of Pennsylvania was never entirely clear—resulted in riots in July, followed by armed resistance to the Government's tax collection efforts. Pursuing a cautious policy to insure that public opinion unequivocally supported his administration's actions, Washington made repeated peace overtures to the rebels. By organizing, temporizing, and rejecting the President's peace offers, the rebels shifted most of the blame for the military action that was to follow onto their own shoulders. With riots elsewhere in Pennsylvania and in Maryland indicating that the rebellion was spreading, the time for action had come. On September 9, the President ordered out over 12,000 militia from Pennsylvania, New Jersey, Maryland, and Virginia. Washington himself took command. Many of the nation's most distinguished leaders and military heroes of the American Revolution occupied important subordinate posts. Even the opposition Republican party newspaper came out with a strong endorsement of military suppression. In the face of that kind of pressure, the whiskey rebels evaporated. The laws were upheld, the insurrection was suppressed, and an important precedent strengthening the authority of the Federal Government was set.[50]

The strong show of force used to crush the Whiskey Rebellion was essential, Washington observed, because "we had given no testimony to the World of being able or willing to support our government and laws."[51] Taken together with the victory over the British-advised Indians, the feverish preparations to erect coastal defenses, and the effort to build a navy, the "testimony" was apparently enough to convince the British that rapprochement with the United States was desirable. In a treaty that Chief Justice of the Supreme Court John Jay negotiated with Foreign Secretary Lord Grenville, the British agreed at last to evacuate British "troops and garrisons from all posts and places within the boundary lines assigned by the [Paris, 1783] treaty of peace to the United States,"[52] and to compensate Americans for ships and cargoes illegally seized in the past. Other provisions of the treaty were less favorable to the United States, and caused a storm of protest throughout the country. Jay, whose hand at the bargaining table had been greatly weakened by Treasury Secretary Alexander Hamilton's pro-British activities, gave more away to Great Britain and obtained less for the United States than his instructions had authorized. Ratification of the treaty eased Anglo-American tensions for a decade and aided Thomas Pinckney in obtaining a favorable treaty with Spain in 1795, which confirmed American Florida boundary claims and navigation rights on the Mississippi. France and Jefferson's Republicans were furious because they saw the treaty as pro-British and anti-French.[53]

For all its very real shortcomings, Jay's Treaty secured for the United States time for continued peaceful development, freedom from territorial encroachments by Great Britain and Spain, a reasonably satisfactory trade agreement with England, and a cautious, decade-long friendship with England. This friendship proved valuable to the nation's tiny fleet during the "Quasi War" with France.

For her part, France meddled in American domestic affairs in 1793 with Citizen Edmond Genêt's† nefarious mission, and attempted to influence the outcome of the 1796 presidential election. Ratification of the Jay Treaty gave France an excuse to step up further her campaign of harassment of American ships at sea in retaliation for the new alliance between her erstwhile ally, the United States, and her ancient enemy, Great Britain. France further insulted the United States by refusing to receive the new American Ambassador, Charles Cotesworth Pinckney in 1796, and with the notorious XYZ Affair** that followed in 1797. These provocations led the United States into open but

---

*An interesting part of this law was the official recognition given to the grade of "cadet." Each company of artillerists and engineers was authorized two cadets.

†Genêt came to the United States in 1793 as Minister from France. He became a factor in the political struggle between Jefferson and Hamilton, and improperly distributed French military commissions to Americans, in anticipation of French military expeditions against Canada and Florida.

**A diplomatic incident involving the American commission that President John Adams sent to France and the ignominious treatment it received.

undeclared naval warfare with France—the "Quasi War" of 1798–1800.

Congress and the Adams administration responded to the crisis precipitated by the French Directory's haughty and venal stance with a flurry of legislation that established a Department of the Navy, augmented the strength of the Navy, established a Marine Corps, strengthened the coastal defenses, and authorized a 10,000-man Provisional Army of federal volunteer troops to be raised for three years' service "in the event of a declaration of war against the United States, . . . actual invasion . . . or of imminent danger of such invasion . . . ." Ex-President George Washington was to be the commander of the Provisional Army when it took the field, but since the French Army was busy looting Europe at the time, President John Adams knew that the chances of the Provisional Army being called to active service to repel invasion were slight. Accordingly, recruitment for this paper army never really got underway. The construction of the coastal defenses,which had been proceeding slowly since 1794, got renewed support from the addition of a second regiment of artillerists and engineers to the permanent military establishment. The First System of Seacoast Defenses, which was composed of primarily Vauban-type fortifications, entered a second phase on a better footing for both construction and manning.[54]

President Adams, beset by strife among the Federalists, and factionalism at home, was able to negotiate an end to the "Quasi War" with Napoleon Bonaparte, who in the meantime had wrested control of France from the Directory by coup d'état. Adams and the divided Federalists were swept from office by the Jeffersonian Republican victory in the election of 1800. The period of Federalist rule, however, had given the United States both its basic military structure and its basic military policy for the next century.

Structurally, both the War and Navy departments had been established as Cabinet posts under the President. The small Army would be maintained in peacetime to police the western frontier and to build and preserve the seacoast fortifications. The Navy, also tiny, would be kept up to protect commerce and demonstrate national resolve on the seas. State militia forces would be used to suppress insurrection and repulse the first blows of any enemy, while the Regulars assembled and trained federal volunteers for longer service than the three-month militia. In summary, the basic military policy of the United States was defensive. In a major war, loosely organized and ill-equipped militia would constitute the nation's main fighting force.

Mr. Jefferson's Army and the Road to War

During the previous decade, Jeffersonian Republicans had maligned the standing army as being dangerous to liberty, and had touted the essential economy and virtue of the militia. Once in office, however, the Jeffersonians kept virtually intact the basic military institutions the Federalists had built. Indeed, they strengthened the standing forces when and as the situation required. No real reform or strengthening of the militia took place, despite frequent calls for cosmetic reform by the administration. By 1801, Jefferson and his party, in spite of the rhetoric, had come to accept a standing force as necessary and useful, even in peacetime. That rhetoric, however, was real to the extent that they did not fear the standing army as much as they feared—and perhaps with some justification—a Federalist standing army. Early in the Jefferson administration, the Army had been purged of its staunchest Federalists by the simple expedient of reducing its size. The staunch Federalists who remained were left with a simple choice: be quiet or resign. More moderate Federalists became the targets of efforts designed to win them over to the Republican cause. For those who persisted in the Federalist persuasion, assignments to dreary or unpromising posts were arranged. It is clear that the officer corps that remained after the reduction of 1802 was acutely aware that "correct political sentiments" were essential to continued success in the peacetime establishment.[55]

John Adams

Not all the officers of the Army that Jefferson inherited from the Adams administration were Federalists. Some were identified as Republican and, as expected, few of this group were discharged in the June 1802 reduction. Others were noted on the Republican's list of officers as "professionally the soldier without any political creed." For both the military and the civil service, the Jeffersonians recognized, however, that finding qualified men with acceptable political beliefs was not always easy. The Federalists had the advantage because, on the average, they were richer and more likely to have college educations. To break their upper-class monopoly on public office, something had to be done to break their upper-class monopoly on education. To open the commissioned ranks of the Army to all classes of citizens, to replace the aristocracy of birth and wealth in the Army with the natural aristocracy of talent and virtue, and to use good men who lacked the advantages of wealth and position, the Jeffersonians determined that they would have to provide the education and training requisite for sound leadership. "The new establishment of republicanism in the army," historian Theodore J. Crackel has observed, "necessitated a military academy."[56]

Jefferson and the Republicans had vigorously opposed previous attempts by Washington, Knox, Hamilton, and others to create a military academy. In office at last, the Republicans were no longer concerned that such an establishment would perpetuate the kind of an army they would have to fear. With the control of appointments for both instructors and cadets in Republican hands, they could be assured that the military academy would train young men of good Republican stock for officership under Republican officers, or at least under non-aristocratic professionals.[57] Near the end of his term, John Adams had used existing laws to appoint a small group of artillery cadets. He had arranged for 10 of them to receive formal instruction in mathematics, artillery, and fortification. Jefferson adopted this little group of young Adams' appointees, and within a scant two and a half months of his inauguration ordered the "immediate" creation of a more formal and permanent academy. Less than a year later, in the very same bill that reduced the Army and helped purge it of its Federalist officers, the United States Military Academy at West Point, New York, received formal legislative approval. It is pertinent to note, however, that the initial academy was not designed to educate all officers; it was simply a small part of a new branch of the Army—the Corps of Engineers. Jefferson, a warm friend of science, willingly supported an institution with a technical flavor, but was still suspicious of an aristocratic, professional officer corps. While legislative machinery was working to produce its sanction for the Military Academy, the executive branch was at work selecting the site for the academy (West Point), ordering the cadets to report there, choosing an appropriate superintendent (Jonathan Williams), selecting qualified teachers, and examining the military and political qualifications of the officer corps. The Military Academy and the reduction of the Army were part of the same plan to shape a safe Republican standing army.[58]

The implementation of Jefferson's military program was aided by the fact that he took office during a period of relaxed tensions with both Great Britain and France. The relaxed international scene allowed a safe reduction in the regular establishment of both the Army and the Navy. Economy was an important part of the total Jeffersonian program, and the smaller Army Jefferson kept had to be utilitarian. When rumors of Spain's transference of Louisiana to the control of Napoleonic France were confirmed, Jefferson talked of mobilizing the militia, but Secretary of War Henry Dearborn shifted the Regulars away from the Northwest and the Atlantic seaboard into the Southwest to counter any threat that might arise as a result of Louisiana's new landlord. When James Monroe's negotiating efforts in Paris unexpectedly left the United States in possession of all of Louisiana, the Army provided expeditionary forces to explore and take possession of the new territory.[59] *(See Map 16.)*

In 1805, the year of Napoleon's victories at Ulm and Austerlitz, warfare in Europe resumed with a vengeance. For the next 10 years, Napoleon's greed, fed by the roar of cannon and the rumble of armies, would allow the Continent no lasting peace. As the Corsican's *Grande Armée* set out to rape and pillage, both England and France resumed their violations of American shipping rights on the high seas. On no point were the Americans more sensitive than their right to use the oceans freely; and on no point were they more ill-prepared to defend their rights in 1805. Beginning their administration as the "Quasi War" ended, the Jeffersonians had reduced the Navy and sold off or laid up the fleet that had acquitted itself so well against the French. Lethargy had overtaken the improvements of the coastal fortifications, as the Army had its main efforts redirected toward the Louisiana frontier. In keeping with the defensive nature of America's overall military policy, Jefferson had preferred to rely on a sort of naval militia—small gunboats—for coastal defense.

By closing the ports of the entire European continent to British trade, Napoleon's Berlin Decrees of November 1806 attempted to establish the only type of blockade a land power could master against England. The Berlin Decrees were an important step along the way to war between the United States and Great Britain. As a result of Lord Nelson's stunning victory over the combined French and

Spanish fleets at Trafalgar a year earlier, the French were actually instituting only a paper blockade, and were in fact unable to interfere any longer with American ships at sea. The victorious Royal Navy, on the other hand, was now free to range the oceans of the world, enforcing the Orders in Council that the British issued in January 1807 in response to Napoleon's Berlin edict. The 1807 orders blockaded the French and forbade neutrals from trading with or between ports under French control. A British squadron took station at the mouth of Chesapeake Bay, flouting American sovereignty by roaming the bay and interfering with commerce at will. Tensions, which had been mounting steadily since 1805, reached crisis proportions in June 1807 when *HMS Leopard* stopped and searched the American frigate *Chesapeake* off Hampton Roads. *(See Map 16.)* When the *Chesapeake*, which was not manned for action, refused to surrender alleged British deserters among her crew, the *Leopard* opened fire, killing three, wounding twenty, and forcibly removing four American seamen. The American public was outraged; public opinion demanded war. Determined to avoid war, Jefferson attempted to quell the crisis through negotiation, meanwhile taking stock of the nation's defenses. The intransigence of the two governments doomed the negotiations to failure from the start. Dealing from relative military weakness, Jefferson responded at last with his own economic warfare: an embargo. In essence, the embargo surrendered the seas to others and forbade American exports. The effect of this action abroad was slight. At home, however, economic disorder and domestic alienation from the Government were the result. But war was temporarily averted, and time was purchased to strengthen American forces. Jefferson supported legislation that nearly tripled the size of the Army in 1808, increased appropriations for coastal defense, and established appropriations for arming the militia.[60]

The Second System of Seacoast Defenses was undertaken in 1807. This system was the first designed and constructed entirely by American officers. Vauban-style designs had been in vogue for seacoast forts in the United States through 1802. That style had been inspired by the French engineers who aided the American cause during the American Revolution and sought refuge and employment in America during the era of the French Revolution. As the "Quasi War" tensions and Jefferson's Republican policies caused the Frenchmen to be discharged and replaced by Americans, a new system was developed through the efforts of the Military Philosophical Society under Colonel Jonathan Williams, the first superintendent of the United States Military Academy. Based on the work of another French engineer, Marc René, Marquis de Montalembert, the new theory abandoned the bastioned trace of Vauban for the

Colonel Jonathan Williams

tenaille trace, a series of triangular redans joined at right angles to form a defensive front resembling the teeth of a saw. The idea was to make better use of improved, longer-range, and more accurate cannon than the close-in defenses provided by the Vauban system.[61]

President Jefferson bequeathed to his successor, James Madison, the defensive military policy that Jefferson had inherited from John Adams. Jefferson, however, had added gunboats, changed the political and social character of the officer corps, and legally established the Military Academy as a source of technically competent engineer officers. He had also spelled out the essence of his defensive policy in his messages to Congress. "The first object," he said in 1805, "is to place our seaport towns out of danger of insult." Heavy cannon and mortars for land batteries, in both fixed fortifications and mobile field batteries, were furnished to achieve this aim. In aid of these batteries, a "considerable" number of gunboats were provided for the protection of the ports and harbors. Jefferson estimated that the militia, "or volunteers instead of them" ("Upward of 300,000 ablebodied men between 18 and 26 years"), would "furnish a competent number for offense or defense in any point where they may be wanted, and will give time for raising regular forces . . . ." The Atlantic was still a defensive moat, giving the nation sufficient warning time to allow it to cling to a passive defense. In its rawest terms, Jefferson's policy for guarding against war with European powers was to defend key ports and harbors with forts and gunboats;

the militia would garrison the threatened forts and absorb the first shocks of any invasion; behind this shield, the Regulars would create the land forces necessary to deal with the invaders.[62]

Jefferson's passive policy was fine for a nation determined to avoid war at all costs. As naval incidents increased and tensions mounted during the next few years, however, the "War Hawks" gained more influence, and the nation began to pursue a foreign policy that was too aggressive to be adequately supported by the traditional military policy and structure.

The War of 1812

The second war with Great Britain has been called the Incredible War of 1812, and with good reason. No new major incidents precipitated the declaration of war in 1812; rather, it resulted from a lengthy buildup of tensions and frustrations, as the Royal Navy showed haughty disregard of American rights at sea, and the British continued arming and inciting the Indians on the western frontier. On June 1, 1812, the President's war message to Congress listed four main charges against the British. All four had to do with American rights at sea, but the maritime states were opposed to war. The western, landlocked states were the home of the most vigorous "War Hawks" of 1812, but the British encouragement of the Indians was only mentioned by Madison as an afterthought.[63] Had war been declared by Jefferson in the wake of the *Chesapeake* affair of 1807, a united country would have supported the redress of such a flagrant insult to the national honor. The embargo on American trade that he imposed instead harmed the Americans worse than the British or French, and divided the country. Maritime New England, hurt most by the embargo, blamed Jefferson and his party more than England for its troubles, while the rest of the country nursed its indignation against Great Britain. True, the embargo had bought time to better prepare the country's defenses, but little had been done to prepare for the aggressive land war that Madison and the Democratic-Republicans were about to unleash.

By the time war was declared on June 18, 1812, the Second System of Seacoast Defenses was essentially complete, but the strength of the Army and Navy was ludicrously small for a nation about to challenge the world's greatest sea power. The Navy had only 20 ships, none larger than the three 44-gun frigates of the "Quasi War." The next in size were three 36-gun frigates, followed by 14 smaller sloops, brigs, and schooners. The Army numbered less than 7,000

officers and men in June of 1812, although its authorized strength had been set at 35,603 in January. About 5,000 additional recruits were available under the authority granted to the President in February and April, if one wished to include volunteers enlisted for shorter periods than the standard five-year term. The President was also empowered by the April legislation to require state governors to keep in readiness about 80,000 militia. Militia, however, could be used only for 90 days a year, and only for defense within the United States.[64]

England considered the war with the United States a minor annoyance when compared with the problem of dealing with Napoleon. Most British resources and forces were fully committed to the much larger war raging in Europe. Only what could be spared from that contest would be employed against the United States. Thus, while the imbalance of force was not as great as it could have been, it was, nonetheless, considerable. There were 7,000 British and Canadian Regulars in Canada, plus as many as 3,500 Indian warriors and perhaps 10,000 Canadian militia. By September, the Royal Navy had 11 ships of the line, 34 frigates, and about 34 smaller craft arrayed against the United States in the western Atlantic.[65] Aware of the "War Hawks" clamoring for the capture of England's provinces, Canadians took the war more seriously and considered it a fight for survival against naked aggression.[66]

American leaders brought a divided United States into war, with no strategy for conducting that war in mind. A general consensus on the objective seems to have been attained, but no real thought or analysis was given to developing plans to achieve the objective using available resources. No one seems to have assessed what those resources really were. Such consensus as there was on an objective seems to have been exactly what the Canadians feared: the United States, in order to punish Great Britain for her disregard of American rights at sea, would conquer Canada. As an adjunct to this effort, an attempt would be made to interdict British commerce on the high seas. Just how these objectives were to be realized was an issue not realistically addressed, because the United States had neither an offensive doctrine nor anyone trained to deal with problems of strategy. The strategic problems since 1776 had been mainly defensive. Such officers as the regular establishment retained in peacetime were concerned with coastal defense or in dealings with the Indians. (James Wilkinson, the Army's senior officer, seems to have been more preoccupied with profit, peculation, and politics than anything else.) The "War Hawks" thought that the militia could easily conquer upper Canada. One braggart even boasted that the militia of Kentucky alone was equal to the entire job of conquering Canada. Such optimistic bombast overlooked two facts: the

Brigadier General James Wilkinson

nation was divided on the war question, and the militia—amateur soldiers organized for defense and the repulsion of invasions—might object and legally refuse to serve in offensive operations outside of the United States. The Navy was to be augmented only by issuing letters of marque to privateers.[67]

The year 1812 was not a good one for the Yankees. Canada's population was located primarily in long thin strips along the St. Lawrence River and the Great Lakes. Seizing Montreal would give the attackers at least two advantages: it would sever the waterway that was Canada's highway and main line of communication; and it would cut western Canada off from aid from either England or the more populous eastern Canada, making the conquest of western Canada relatively easy. Instead of massing their forces for an attack on Montreal, the Americans mounted four separate, uncoordinated offensives in 1812. *(See Map 17.)* Michigan Territorial Governor William Hull, an aging, infirm, and now timid veteran of the Revolution, led the first attack against Canada from Detroit. Hull's offensive was thwarted by his own bumbling, and finally decisively countered by Major General Isaac Brock, military commander and civil Governor of upper Canada. Leading a small force of Canadian militia, British Regulars, and Indians, he captured Detroit and the unfortunate Hull. In October, militia Major General Stephen Van Rensselaer's assault across the Niagara River on Queenstown was re-

pulsed by Brock, when most of Van Rensselaer's militiamen refused to cross the river and Brigadier General Alexander Smyth ignored Van Rensselaer's pleas for help from the Regulars. In November, ex-Secretary of War, Major General Henry Dearborn, another veteran of the Revolution, led an abortive attempt on Montreal along the most promising route of advance into Canada. When his advance guard was repulsed just over the border by Canadian militia and Indians, his New York and Vermont volunteers refused to leave American soil. Dearborn marched back to winter quarters in Plattsburg. The fourth assault, which was supposed to be mounted from Sacket's Harbor, never got underway.[68]

America's understanding of strategy fared little better in 1813 than it had in 1812. While Secretary of War John Armstrong was supplying Dearborn for operations against Canada, Brigadier General William H. Harrison, the Governor of Indiana Territory who had proved himself a competent Indian fighter in November 1811 at Tippecanoe, made several unsuccessful attempts to retake Detroit during the winter of 1812–1813. *(See Map 18.)* This action against Detroit was supposed to pin down the British in the west, while Dearborn dealt with Canada farther to the east. Only after Commodore Oliver Hazard Perry defeated the British squadron on Lake Erie in September was American control over the Northwest reasserted. Once in complete control of the lake, Perry ferried Harrison's troops across. Having thus turned the British positions at Detroit and Fort

Major General William H. Harrison

Malden, the Americans caught up with the retreating British near Moravian Town on the banks of the Thames River and whipped them soundly.[69]

Harrison's victory on the Thames together with Perry's control of Lake Erie ended the fighting in that sector for the rest of the war. The Americans there, in addition to securing control of the lake, had re-established the Detroit frontier, brought a portion of western Canada under American control, and smashed the Indian confederacy that supported the British.[70]

To the east, the Yankees fared less well. Secretary of War Armstrong had developed a promising campaign plan for dealing with eastern Canada in 1813. This plan envisioned the capture of Kingston on Lake Ontario *(see Map 18)* as the primary objective for Dearborn's forces. Capture of Kingston, American naval strategist Alfred Thayer Mahan observed later, would solve "at a single stroke every difficulty" in this theater. "No other harbor was tenable as a naval station; with its fall and destruction of shipping and forts, would go the control of the lake, even if the place itself were not permanently held. Deprived thus of the water communications, the enemy could retain no position to the westward, because neither reinforcements nor supplies could reach them." Armstrong's plan established York (now Toronto) as Dearborn's second objective. As his third task, Dearborn was to cooperate with a force from Buffalo in securing the Canadian shore of the Niagara River.[71]

Dearborn and Commodore Isaac Chauncey, the American naval commander on Lake Ontario, discussed their fears that Kingston would be strongly defended, and thus requested a change in the plan. Dearborn displayed the bankruptcy of American strategic doctrine and training by proposing to attack Kingston only after York and the Niagara forts had fallen. Incredibly, Armstrong approved, thus demonstrating that he too lacked the moral courage, singleness of purpose, and sense of objective that in the same year marked Napoleon and Wellington as great battle captains.[72]

After some initial success, Dearborn's offensive collapsed. At the end of April, Dearborn's men, commanded in the field by renowned explorer Brigadier General Zebulon Pike, successfully raided York. Pike was among the heavy casualties suffered by both sides in this pointless raid. The displaced British predictably retreated to Kingston, bolstering the enemy forces there for a later counterblow. A month after beginning the York raid, Dearborn mounted a well executed amphibious assault, led by Colonel Winfield Scott, across the Niagara River. Dearborn's failure to follow up the success of this assault with a vigorous pursuit destroyed the chance for a complete victory. The British recovered their balance and twice defeated larger American con-

tingents, causing Dearborn's offensive to fizzle out. Dearborn fizzled out with it. The President relieved him in July.[73]

While Dearborn's forces occupied themselves on the Niagara frontier, Sir George Prevost, the Governor General of Canada, sent his own amphibious assault against Sacket's Harbor, using forces he had assembled at Kingston—including about 250 men displaced from York and 800 British Regulars. Brigadier General Jacob Brown of the New York militia made good use of 400 Regulars and 750 militia in repulsing this British counterblow.[74]

America's last offensive gasp in the east for 1813 was made in the fall, with a belated two-pronged attack on Montreal. *(See Map 18.)* James Wilkinson, now a major general, replaced Dearborn and led one of the attacking columns to humiliating defeat near Christler's Farm at the hands of a smaller British force. Operating under the command of Major General Wade Hampton, who lacked confidence in either Wilkinson or the War Department, the other column retreated all the way to Plattsburg and winter quarters at first contact with the enemy. Wilkinson made his last shameful appearance on the battlefield in March 1814. His attack, waged by 4,000 men, was repulsed by 200 Canadian and British troops near La Colle Mill.[75]

Elsewhere in 1813, the Americans opened a new theater of operations in the South by occupying that part of west Florida that had been in dispute between Spain and the United States. Andrew Jackson, commander of the Tennessee militia, began a campaign against the Creek Indians that lasted until the spring of 1814 and won Jackson an appointment as a Regular Army major general. The British, for their part, sponsored a series of punitive raids along the Chesapeake under Admiral George Cockburn.

The last year of the war (1814) was characterized by British offensives and American successes. *(See Map 19.)* After Wilkinson's March departure freed the Army of the last of its incompetent commanders, the Americans began to rely on younger, proven battle captains. Militia General Jacob Brown received Regular Army brigadier stars for his victory at Sacket's Harbor; he was made a major general in 1814, and given command of the Niagara district. Winfield Scott, contentious prewar Regular but now a brigadier as a reward for his aggressive service in 1813, arrived in March of 1814 to command one of Brown's brigades. With Brown's blessing, Scott established a camp of instruction that between March and the end of June drilled and trained the units of Brown's army into an effective, hard-fighting outfit. On July 3, Brown sent his forces to capture Fort Erie. That success was followed quickly by Scott's victory over a slightly larger British force under Major General Phinneas Riall at Chippewa, where the more accurate and

The Battle of Chippewa, July 1814: "Those are Regulars, by God"

destructive musketry and artillery fire of Scott's well-trained force made the difference. Later in July, Scott's training methods again paid dividends when Brown and Scott fought the British at Lundy's Lane. If Lundy's Lane was at worst a draw, the Americans ever after would remember it as a victory.[76]

Temporarily relieved from the French threat with Napoleon's downfall in April of 1814, the British began to rush forces from Europe to deal with the troublesome Yankees in North America. Changing from a defensive strategy to an offensive one, they contemplated staging operations against the American coasts and attacks out of Canada to conquer large areas of American territory "to obtain if possible ultimate security to His Majesty's Possessions in America."[77]

Pursuant to this strategy, Prevost attacked south toward Plattsburg. *(See Map 19.)* Crossing the border on September 1, he arrived opposite Plattsburg on the sixth with perhaps 11,000 troops, including many grizzled veterans of the Napoleonic Wars. There he waited for a week for naval support. Facing this fearsome array was a small American force of 4,500 Regulars, volunteers, and militia under one of the new brigadiers of 1814, Alexander Macomb, a promising young army engineer. More important, as events were to prove, the Americans also had a small fleet under Commodore Thomas Macdonough. Macdonough's well-trained seamen and gunners battered an equal but less well-trained British flotilla into submission. Noting Macdonough's victory on the lake—and perhaps remembering Burgoyne's unhappy fate in 1777—Prevost, to

the dismay of those who had served with Wellington, cancelled his land attack, folded his tents, and returned to Canada.[78]

Throughout 1814, the British launched raids along the Chesapeake at will. They routed the Regulars and militia protecting Washington and burned the Capitol, the White House, and other public buildings. *(See Map 19.)* Another force of Regulars and militia, however, repulsed a British attack on Baltimore two days after Macdonough's victory on Lake Champlain.[79] The British then moved to the Gulf coast, hoping to capture New Orleans and possibly gain Louisiana. *(See Map 20.)* Peninsula veteran Major General Sir Edward Pakenham took charge of the British operations on the Mississippi River on Christmas Day, 1814. After being bested by the Americans in an artillery duel on January 1, 1815, Pakenham elected to conduct a frontal assault on Major General Andrew Jackson's position. He also directed that a 600-man force cross the river and launch an attack on the west bank to clear American artillery positions in which guns were sited for the purpose of protecting Jackson's earthworks with supporting fire. Pakenham's main attack on January 6 was repulsed, with appalling losses inflicted by heavy American artillery fire that consisted of grape and cannister, which shredded the British massed formations. Infantrymen firing rifles and muskets blindly into the smoke and mist of the early dawn from behind the barricades also took their toll. When the smoke finally cleared, Pakenham had been killed and his force shattered. On February 8, the British survivors salvaged their pride by overwhelming Fort Bowyer, a post defended by 350 Regulars, at the mouth of

Mobile Harbor. Before Mobile itself could be attacked, word arrived that a peace treaty had been signed at Ghent on Christmas Eve, the day before Pakenham had arrived to take charge of the ill-fated attempt on New Orleans.[80]

The end of the war was as odd as its beginning. With the joyous news of the victory at New Orleans arriving almost simultaneously with the news of the Treaty of Ghent, Americans quickly and conveniently confused the facts in their minds and began to think that they had won the War of 1812. It had not been won. Concluded by a negotiated peace, it was at best a draw. None of the original goals of the war had been achieved: Great Britain had not been compelled to repeal her Orders in Council unconditionally or to change her imposed rules for the use of the sealanes when she was at war; Canada remained safely in British hands; and American commerce raiders had been effectively blockaded in the harbors after the first year of the war. War weary from a generation of difficult wars with France and Napoleon, and unable to muster any support at home for an increasingly unpopular war with the United States, the British Government was more than happy to conclude the affair. The American Government, which had been thwarted in its attempts to conquer Canada and had faced possible secession on the part of New England, also was happy to gain a peace that left the country intact.

By analyzing the course of the war, America learned many lessons. Unfortunately, some of the lessons were in conflict with others. The Regulars had done as well—and as poorly—as the militia during the early phase of the war. When properly trained and ably led, both the militia and the Regulars had done well. The Regulars could point with pride to Chippewa and Lundy's Lane, and view with alarm the New York militia's refusal to invade Canada in 1812 and the "Bladensburg Races" before Washington in 1814; however, the militia could point with pride to the defense of Baltimore and New Orleans, and view with equal alarm Smyth's refusal of aid to Van Rensselaer and James Wilkinson's lengthy catalog of faults. The Artillery and Engineers had done unexpectedly well. At Chippewa, Sackett's Harbor, Norfolk, Baltimore, and New Orleans, the skill of the gunners had been a major factor in American successes. The Corps of Engineers displayed the talents of the young Military Academy graduates in fortification. Academy men took just pride in the fortifications at places like Fort Erie, Fort Meigs, and Plattsburg. The excellent leadership demonstrated by Brown, Jackson, and Scott showed that neither the Regulars nor the citizen-soldiers had a monopoly in this area. But if leadership and training had begun to pay dividends by 1814, strategic direction and doctrine had remained bankrupt. Education in the principles of strategy was lacking still, and the problem of raising an army, as opposed to improvising one in the face of the enemy, remained unresolved as the nation turned again to internal development.

Notes

[1]John Shy, *A People Numerous & Armed* (New York, 1976), p. 234.

[2]*Ibid.*, p. 235.

[3]Shy, *People*, pp. 234-238; Douglas Edward Leach, *Arms for Empire; A Military History of the British Colonies in North America, 1607-1763* (New York, 1973), pp. 1ff; Russell F. Weigley, *History of the United States Army* (New York, 1967), p. 3.

[4]Leach, *Arms*, p. 52.

[5]*Ibid.*, p. 10; Shy, *People*, pp. 233-238.

[6]Shy, *People*, pp. 26-27; Leach, *Arms*, pp. 55-56.

[7]Material and ideas on the remainder of this section are drawn from: Shy, *People*, pp. 24-33, 195-254; Leach, *Arms*, pp. 1-115; Richard H. Kohn, *Eagle and Sword: The Federalists and the Creation of the Military Establishment in America, 1783-1802* (New York, 1975, pp. 1-13; Shy, *Toward Lexington; The Role of the British Army in the Coming of the American Revolution* (Princeton, 1965), *passim*; Don Higginbotham, *The War of American Independence: Military Attitudes, Policies, and Practice, 1763-1789* (New York, 1971), pp. 1-77; Theodore Ropp, *War in the Modern World*, Revised edition (New York, 1965), pp. 76-93; Marcus Cunliffe, *Soldiers & Civilians: The Martial Spirit in America, 1775-1865* (Boston, 1968), pp. 31-43; Walter Millis, *Arms and Men: A Study in American Military History* (New York, 1956), pp. 34-35.

[8]See Howard Peckham, *Toll of Independence* (Chicago, 1974), *passim* for locations of militia actions throughout the war.

[9]A useful discussion of money matters in this period is found in E. James Fergusson, *The Power of the Purse* (Chapel Hill, 1961), *passim;* see especially pp. 109-124, 140-146, 171-176. As a general guide for the Confederation period the author relied upon Edmund S. Morgan's chapters in John M. Blum, et al., *The National Experience: A History of the United States*, 4th edition (New York, 1977), and Kohn, *Eagle*, pp. 17-88.

[10]Quoted in Kohn, *Eagle*, p. 42 from Madison, "Notes on Debates," April 4, 1783, *Papers of John Madison*, VI, 433.

[11]On consensus point see: John McAuley Palmer, *America in Arms* (New Haven, 1941), pp. 6-7; Kohn, *Eagle*, pp. 42-43; and Walter Millis, *American Military Thought* (New York, 1966), pp. 16-17.

[12]Palmer, *Arms*, p.7.

[13]Washington's "Sentiments on a Peace Establishment" are found reprinted in a number of places. The quotations used here are from Appendix I, John McAuley Palmer, *Washington, Lincoln, Wilson;. Three War Statesmen* (Garden City, N.Y., 1930).

[14]Kohn, *Eagle*, pp. 40-62; Lawrence D. Cress, "The Standing Army, The Militia, and the New Republic; Changing Attitudes Toward the Military in American Society, 1768 to 1820," unpublished Ph.D. dissertation, University of Virginia, 1976, pp. 194-234; Maurice Matloff (ed.), *American Military History* (Washington, 1969), pp. 103-104.

[15]*Journals of the Continental Congress,* XXVII, 524, 538-540, 551-553; quotation is from p. 538.

[16]Morgan, *Experience*, p. 119; Max Farrand, *Records of the U.S. Constitutional Convention*, III, 543-550; J. Mackay Hitsman, *The Incredible War of 1812* (Toronto, 1965), p. 4.

[17]Morgan, *Experience*, p. 119; Merrill Jensen, *The New Nation* (New York, 1967), pp. 169-170, 174; Farrand, *Records*, III, 547-548.

[18]Morgan, *Experience*, pp. 119-120; Jensen, *Nation*, pp. 170-174.

[19]Matloff, *Military History*, p. 110; James Ripley Jacobs, *The Beginning of the U.S. Army, 1783-1812* (Princeton, 1947), pp. 13-39; Kohn, *Eagle*, pp. 51, 54-72; Francis Paul Prucha, *The Sword of the Republic; The United States Army on the Frontier, 1783-1846* (New York, 1969), pp. 6-15; Joseph Parker Warren, "The Confederation and the Shays' Rebellion," *The American Historical Review*, XI (October, 1905), 51-56; Higginbotham, *War*, pp. 445-447.

[20]Farrand, *Records*, II, 332.

[21]Warren, "Shays'," pp. 42-43, 45-46; Kohn, *Eagle*, p. 74; Cress, "Army and Militia," pp. 237-238; Jensen, *Nation*, pp. 308-310; Higginbotham, *War*, pp. 447-448.

[22]Higginbotham, *War*, pp. 447-448;. Kohn, *Eagle*, p. 74; Warren, "Shays'," pp. 45-46, 60.

[23]Warren, "Shays'," pp. 43, 51-56; Higginbotham, *War*, p. 448; Weigley, *History*, p. 48; Matloff, *Military History*, p. 105;. Millis, *Arms*, p. 47.

[24]Farrand, *Records*, III, 539-549, gives Madison's list of problems leading to the Constitution, calling them "diseases" on p. 549. Quotation is from Walter Millis, *Arms*, p. 47.

[25]Farrand, *Records*, II, 329-333, 386-388, 616-617; III, 207, 318-319, 420-421; U.S. Constitution, Article I, Section 8; Article II, Section 2; Article IV, Section 4; Amendments II, IX, & X.

[26]U.S. Constitution, Articles I & II.

[27]Farrand, *Records*, II, 331-332, 387, 388.

[28]Edmund Randolph in Farrand, *Records*, II, 387.

[29]Elbridge Gerry of Massachusetts in *Annals of Congress*, I, 778.

[30]See, for example, the large number of the *Federalist Papers* devoted to the military clauses.

[31]Washington, "Sentiments"; Knox's 1790 plan is found in *American State Papers, Military Affairs*, I, 6-13 hereafter cited as *ASP, MA*; Kohn, *Eagle*, p. 86.

[32]Kohn, *Eagle*, p. 87.

[33]*ASP, MA*, I, 6-13; Weigley, *History*, pp. 88-90; John K. Mahon, *The American Militia; Decade of Decision, 1789-1800*, University of Florida Monographs: Social Sciences, No. 6, Spring 1960 (Gainesville, 1960), pp. 14-15.

[34]Jacobs, *U.S. Army*, pp. 50-53; Weigley, *History*, p. 90. On Indian belligerence and white demands see especially Kohn, *Eagle*, pp. 96-102.

[35]Jacobs, *U.S. Army*, pp. 53-60; Weigley, *History*, p. 91.

[36]Weigley, *History*, pp. 90-91.

[37]Jacobs, *U.S. Army*, pp. 85-122; Kohn, *Eagle*, pp. 111-116.

[38]John F. Callan, *The Military Laws of the United States* (Baltimore, 1858), p. 63.

[39]Mahon, *Militia*, pp. 14-21; Thomas Hart Benton (ed.), *Abridgement of Congressional Debates (New York, 1857), pp.* 341-350; Callan, *Laws*, pp. 64-70; Kohn, *Eagle*, pp. 128-138.

[40]Emory Upton, *The Military Policy of the United States* (Washington, 1904), p. 85; Palmer, *Washington*, pp. 130-135;

Palmer, *Arms*, pp. 50–55; Kohn, *Eagle*, pp. 135–138.

⁴¹Weigley, *History*, p. 94.

⁴²Kohn, *Eagle*, pp. 124–127; Weigley, *History*, p. 92.

⁴³Kohn, *Eagle*, pp. 125–126; Jacobs, *U.S. Army*, pp. 126–127; Weigley, *History*, pp. 92–93.

⁴⁴Jacobs, *U.S. Army*, pp. 124–152; Weigley, *History*, pp. 92–93.

⁴⁵The best accessible account of the Battle of Fallen Timbers is found in Jacobs, *U.S. Army*, pp. 153–188; also see Kohn, *Eagle*, pp. 156–157; Weigley, *History*, p. 93; Hitsman, *Incredible War*, p. 11.

⁴⁶See, for example, Washington's address to the Joint Session of Congress, Dec. 3, 1793, and his message to Congress, Dec. 5, 1793, *Annals of the Congress of the United States, 3d Congress*, pp. 11–13, 15–16. Many other pages of this volume are devoted to questions of commerce at sea and appropriate defenses (e.g., 155–158, 174–247, 250f, 1303–1307).

⁴⁷Arthur P. Wade, "Artillerists and Engineers: The Beginnings of American Seacoast Fortifications, 1794–1815," unpublished Ph.D. dissertation, Kansas State University, 1977, p. 7.

⁴⁸*Annals*, IV, 1426; Millis, *Arms*, p. 55.

⁴⁹*Annals*, IV, 250, 469, 479–480, 499–500, 1423–1424, 1428–1429, 1444–1445; Wade, "Fortifications," pp. 9–10, 13, 22–23, 27–28. The congressional committee report is found in *ASP, MA*, I, 61–62.

⁵⁰The most interesting interpretive study of the Whiskey Rebellion is found in Kohn, *Eagle*, pp. 157–173; Don Higginbotham, *Daniel Morgan; Revolutionary Rifleman* (Chapel Hill, 1961), pp. 186–198, describes the old war hero's role. Weigley, *History*, pp. 100–102, extends the rebels no sympathy.

⁵¹Quoted in Bernard Bailyn, et al., *The Great Republic: A History of the American People* (Lexington, Mass., 1977), p. 349.

⁵²Quoted in Richard N. Current, et al., *American History: A Survey*, 4th edition (New York, 1975), p. 163.

⁵³The following general histories of the period were consulted on the Jay Treaty: Bailyn, et al., *Great Republic*, pp. 349–350; Blum, et al., *Experience*, pp. 140–142; Current, et al., *American*, pp. 162–163. On rapprochement with the British, see Bradford Perkins, *The First Rapprochement: England and the United States, 1795–1805* (Philadelphia, 1955), pp. 1–6 *passim*.

⁵⁴Wade, "Fortifications," pp. 73–105; Kohn, *Eagle*, pp. 193–272; Jacobs, *U.S. Army*, pp. 221–223; Callan, *Laws*, pp. 85–89; and *Annals*, IX, 3710–3711, 3717, 3721–3733, 3736–3739, 3743–3744, 3747–3749, 3750–3757, 3774–3776, 3785–3789, 3791–3794.

⁵⁵Major Theodore Crackel, unpublished paper, "Mr. Jefferson and the Army: Politics, Reform and the Military Establishment, 1801–1809," delivered at meeting of the Missouri Valley Historical Society, 1977, pp. 8–13, 22–23.

⁵⁶*Ibid.*, pp. 13, 26.

⁵⁷*Ibid.*, pp. 14–15.

⁵⁸*Ibid.*, pp. 14, 16–18; Wade, "Fortifications," pp. 117–125; Callan, *Laws*, p. 106; Thomas E. Griess, "Dennis Hart Mahan:

West Point Professor and Advocate of Military Professionalism, 1830–1871," unpublished Ph.D. dissertation, Duke University, 1968, pp. 60–61.

⁵⁹Wade, "Fortifications," pp. 162–164.

⁶⁰*Ibid.*, pp. 198–221; Thomas Jefferson's messages found in James E. Richardson, (ed.), *A Compilation of the Messages and Papers of the Presidents, 1789–1902* (Washington, 1904), I, 372, 383–386, 395, 410, 419–421, 422–424, 426–428, 433, 445–448, 449, 451–456.

⁶¹Wade, "Fortifications," pp. 186–192.

⁶²Richardson, *Messages*, I, 385, 410, 419.

⁶³*Ibid.*, pp. 499–505.

⁶⁴Hitsman, *Incredible War*, pp. 41–42, Matloff, *Military History*, pp. 123–124.

⁶⁵Matloff, *Military History*, pp. 125–126.

⁶⁶On this point, see Hitsman, *Incredible War*, pp. 1–40, a history of the war written by a Canadian. The aspect of survival against U.S. aggression is an underlying theme of the entire book. Although Hitsman chronicles the British affronts to American sovereignty and their intransigence in redress of real American grievances, a basic assumption he makes is that America wanted to conquer Canada and add it to her domain. He tells how the Canadians, against great odds, survived the threat.

⁶⁷Russell F. Weigley, *American Way of War* (New York, 1973), pp. 40, 46–50; Matloff, *Military History*, pp. 126–127; Millis, *Arms*, pp. 65–70; Hitsman, *Incredible War*, pp. 21–22; Blum, et al., *Experience*, pp. 169–171.

⁶⁸Matloff, *Military History*, pp. 124, 127–130; Weigley, *War*, pp. 47–48; Vincent J. Esposito (ed.), *The West Point Atlas of American Wars* (2 Vols.; New York, 1959), I, 10.

⁶⁹Esposito, *West Point Atlas*, I, 10; Matloff, *Military History*, p. 134.

⁷⁰Matloff, *Military History*, p. 134.

⁷¹Hitsman, *Incredible War*, p. 122; Matloff, *Military History*, p. 131; Esposito, *West Point Atlas*, I, 10.

⁷²Hitsman, *Incredible War*, pp. 122–123; Matloff, *Military History*, p. 131.

⁷³Esposito, *West Point Atlas*, I, 10; Matloff, *Military History*, p. 132; Hitsman, *Incredible War*, pp. 130–131, 134–135, 138–139.

⁷⁴Matloff, *Military History*, p. 132.

⁷⁵Matloff, *Military History*, pp. 134–135, 140; Esposito, *West Point Atlas*, I, 10.

⁷⁶Weigley, *History*, pp. 123, 126–127, 129–130; Esposito, *West Point Atlas*, I, 11; Hitsman, *Incredible War*, pp. 195–196, 198–200.

⁷⁷Bathurst to Prevost, June 3, 1814, reprinted in Hitsman, *Incredible War*, pp. 249–251.

⁷⁸Matloff, *Military History*, pp. 143–144; Hitsman, *Incredible War*, pp. 219–231.

⁷⁹Matloff, *Military History*, p. 143.

⁸⁰John William Ward, *Andrew Jackson; Symbol for an Age* (New York, 1962), pp. 16–29; Matloff, *Military History*, pp. 144–146.

"But For Our Graduated Cadets..."

4

On February 20, 1815, the United States Congress met amid the ashes left by the British sack of the Capital the previous August to read President Madison's February 18 message that transmitted the Treaty of Ghent. Euphoria had been running especially high since the night of February 13, when the express rider brought the treaty with the news that the war was over. In the ensuing week, the lawmakers had spent much time patting themselves on the back for Jackson's victory at New Orleans. The speakers could afford to be lavish, for they knew that they would not have to back their brave words with action. Probably few members of the Congress noticed the irony and hollowness of Madison's congratulations to them and "our constituents upon an event which is highly honorable to the nation, and terminates with peculiar felicity a campaign signalized by the most brilliant successes."[1]

The recollection of the early failures of the war and the burning of Washington, however, were recent enough to cause the Congress and the President to look with some care at the military forces they were about to reduce to peacetime strength. In his February 18 message, Madison urged Congress to "provide for the maintenance of an adequate regular force; for the gradual advancement of the naval establishment; for improving all the means of harbour defense; for adding discipline to the distinguished bravery of the militia, and for cultivating the military art in its essential branches, under the liberal patronage of Government."[2] In keeping with the spirit of nationalism and reform in all areas of American life following the war, Congress heeded Madison's words and did not immediately reduce and then neglect the peacetime military establishment. For the next several years, Congress and the administrations of both James Madison and James Monroe helped to improve the regular military and naval forces. However, the militia—always a hot potato, and now riding the crest of the New Orleans-induced tidal wave of sentiment—was left as it had

been before 1812. Building on the reforms instituted between 1815 and the retrenchment of 1821, the Regular Army evolved into a more professional force. This evolution is the theme of this chapter, which covers the Army's growth from 1815 to the Civil War. During this period of almost a half century, important steps were taken to improve the organization of the War Department and the Army, and the nation gradually adopted a strategy that stressed an increase in the strength of the Navy and the development of a Third System of Seacoast Defenses. Impelled by the doctrine of Manifest Destiny, the United States also fought a war with Mexico.

Organizing for Peace

Prior to 1813, no effective system for administering the Army existed. Fear of a standing army and the scattered locations of small garrisons to protect the frontiers delayed the development of an effective system of supply and administration. Historian Leonard D. White described the system in use from 1802 to 1812 by saying that it "lacked integration, responsibility, unity, and energy, and was utterly inadequate for even the most modest military operations."[3] Difficulties in communication and the lack of a good road system, coupled with the small size of the Army, made it doubtful that a high degree of central direction was possible or, given the Democratic-Republicans' penchant for economy, even desirable. The War Department made do with an accountant and the clerks who copied figures and letters. No central agencies for control existed. But the problems of supply and administration brought on by the War of 1812 were too great for the Secretary of War and 12 clerks to handle. The disasters of 1812 prompted Congress to assist the Secretary and strengthen the Army by providing a general staff. The general staff provided for in 1813 was not a coordinated planning staff, such as that used by the Prussians against Napoleon, but rather a housekeeping staff similar to the modern special staff that is concerned with logistical and personnel matters. Included in this early general staff were: the departments of the Adjutant General, Inspector General, Quartermaster General, Topographical Engineers, Commissary of Ordnance, Hospital, Purchasing and Paymaster; the Judge Advocate; the Chaplain; the Military Academy and the Commanding Generals of the military districts and their staffs. Not all members of the general staff were stationed in Washington, but those who were there provided a management staff to assist the Secretary of War.[4]

Following the war, Congress again considered the question of the staff. In reply to a congressional request for his thoughts on the subject, Secretary of War William H. Crawford replied that the general staff should be maintained in peacetime. "The experience of the first two campaigns of the last war, which has furnished volumes of evidence upon this subject," Crawford wrote, "has incontestably established not only the expediency, but the necessity of giving to the military establishment, in time of peace, the organization which it must have to render it efficient in a state of war."[5] Congress followed his advice; in the spring of 1816, a law was passed that made the general staff departments—later to be called the bureaus—permanent parts of the peacetime establishment.[6]

Just a few days after the act organizing the general staff was passed, Congress provided funds for the militia, the Navy, and the seacoast fortifications. The militia was neither reorganized nor reformed, but it was granted $200,000 per year for arms and equipment. This subsidization, while it did not increase appropriations for the same purpose enacted just before the War of 1812, at least precluded a return entirely to the older 1792 system, which had the militia providing all of its own equipment. Despite periodic attempts to improve its organization and discipline—by Presidents, by Congressmen, and by remonstrances from some state legislatures—the militia would neither be reorganized nor reformed until 1903. For the Navy, $200,000 per year was appropriated to provide for a gradual increase to a strength of nine 74-gun ships of the line and twelve 44-gun frigates. Also included were steam engines to build three steam batteries for port and harbor defense. In addition, $838,000 was appropriated for a major new building program for "permanent" fortification of the coasts.[7]

In April 1816, under Secretary of War Crawford's sponsorship, the United States Military Academy at West Point gained support when Congress appropriated money for

Secretary of War John C. Calhoun

buildings, books, maps, and instruments. The facilities and staff of the academy were expanded, the curriculum was broadened, requirements for admission were improved, and the Board of Visitors was formally established. Cadet gray uniforms were issued for the first time that fall. Tradition has held ever since that the gray was issued to honor the Regulars who fought at Chippewa and Lundy's Lane in rough gray kersey.[8]

Upon Crawford's appointment as Secretary of the Treasury in the fall of 1816, the office of Secretary of War lay vacant for more than a year, as a succession of politicians declined the appointment. Finally, President Monroe offered the job to John C. Calhoun, one of the young "War Hawks" of 1812. An able and ambitious politician and administrator, Calhoun became one of the great Secretaries of War during his eight-year tenure. Seeking to prove his executive competence in his quest for the presidency, Calhoun left his mark on the institution and furthered the development of professionalism in the United States Army.

In 1818, troubles arose involving Indians along the Georgia-Florida border. The commander of the Division of the South, Major General Andrew Jackson, who was always alert for an opportunity to further his military career, assembled a motley force of militia, Tennessee volunteers, friendly Indians, and Regulars to deal with the crisis. Giving the broadest possible interpretation to his instructions, if not blatantly exceeding them, "Old Hickory" used his makeshift army to invade Spanish Florida and punish the Seminoles. In the process he brought the United States to the brink of an even greater crisis by capturing the Spanish posts of St. Marks and Pensacola, deposing the Spanish Governor, and leaving an occupation garrison at each location flying the American flag. While on Spanish soil, he captured, tried, and executed two British subjects, Alexander Arbuthnot and Robert C. Ambrister, for inciting, arming, and training the Indians and runaway slaves, who were the cause of the border trouble. Fortunately, neither Spain nor Great Britain chose to make an issue of Jackson's highhanded conduct. The administration, however, carefully chastised the politically powerful general, whose aggressive conduct had, after all, brought the First Seminole War to a swift conclusion.[9] Only the diplomatic acumen and *sang-froid* of the Secretary of State, John Quincy Adams, who was negotiating with the Spanish Minister, Luis de Onís, at the time, made the best of the bad situation Jackson had created. In the end, Florida was ceded to the United States by the Adams-Onís Treaty of 1819. Jackson's political popularity soared as a result of his invasion. The ratification of the Adams-Onís Treaty and the appointment of Jackson as the first Governor of Florida in 1821 seemed to vindicate the politician-general in the nation's eyes.[10]

Jackson's Florida campaign revealed two main problems with the structure of the Army. Calhoun dealt with the first and the Congress with the second. A breakdown in the sup-

Andrew Jackson

plying of his force had been Jackson's biggest problem on campaign. When civilian contractors failed to meet their obligations, the feeding of his troops took all of Jackson's energies from January until the first contact with the Indians in April. Similar problems with civilian contractors during the War of 1812 had demonstrated to Calhoun and the Army the folly of depending on civilians for such an essential item as rations. Jackson's problems in the Seminole War brought action. In accordance with recommendations made by Calhoun, Congress passed legislation that required contractors to deliver the rations in bulk to depots, where a better system of transportation and a stricter control of quality and distribution would be provided by the Army. A separate Commissary General of Subsistence was appointed to head the Subsistence Department.[11]

The other problem that surfaced during Jackson's Florida campaign involved command of the Army. At the close of the War of 1812, two major generals had been retained, Jacob Brown and Andrew Jackson. Brown commanded the Northern Division and Jackson the Southern. In theory, the major generals commanding the field army were coequally responsible to the President and his agent, the Secretary of War. Since the general staff worked for the Secretary, the field commanders found that they were receiving instructions from the President, the Secretary, and the staff chiefs. Confusion could easily result, especially if a commander like Jackson wanted to use the confusion for his own purposes. Congress, in the process of reducing the Army to 6,000 men as an economy measure in 1820–1821, resolved the problem by allowing only one major general to be retained. The House, motivated in part by a reaction to Jackson's seizure of Florida "not only without orders, but plainly contrary to orders, and, what is worse than all, contrary to the Constitution of the Country," voted at first to retain only a single brigadier, hoping to eliminate "great military chieftains" of such great influence and power that they "may not only violate the Constitution and laws of the country, but, by their influence, bring the Government to support and protect them in this violation." The Senate would not agree to this, however, and the compromise bill finally approved provided for a major general and two brigadier generals.[12]

Calhoun made the best of this congressional fiat by calling to Washington the senior major general, Jacob Brown, to assume the office of the Commanding General of the Army. (Andrew Jackson left the service to become Governor of Florida.) Located at the seat of government, the senior officer could better receive executive direction while commanding the field army. Unfortunately, the duties and responsibilities of the Commanding General were not clear-

Major General Jacob Brown

ly stated by Calhoun when he established the office. The general staff continued to be directly responsible to the Secretary of War and quite independent of the Commanding General. Thus, with administrative functions being directly controlled by the Secretary, the functioning of the office of the Commanding General depended upon the personalities involved and the informal agreements between them. This organizational arrangement was to survive the Civil War; the ambiguities it created would be the basis of considerable friction between the staff and fighting units of the Army, and between the Commanding General and various succeeding administrations.[13]

Calhoun's appointees for the chiefs of the staff bureaus, as they came to be called after 1821, were, in general, vigorous and competent men. George Gibson, selected by Calhoun to head the Subsistence Department, was in his thirties when he received the appointment. Thomas Jesup was chosen to be quartermaster general before he was 30. Such men gave their departments continuity and stability. Jesup served as head of his department for 42 years, and Gibson for 43. This long tenure and stability extended to key subordinates as well, and insured that the departments did a professional job of supporting the line units, "providing they were given adequate planning guidance." It also insured that in time, as they developed a better understanding of their particular staff functions, they would become jealous and protective of their prerogatives.[14]

As Secretary of War, Calhoun felt that education and ex-

perience were important for officers to attain in peacetime, so that they would be properly prepared for war service. "War is an art," Calhoun wrote to the Congress, "to attain perfection in which, much time and experience, particularly for the officers, are necessary . . . . To give to the officers of the army the necessary skill and acquirements, the military academy is an invaluable part of our establishment; but that alone will be inadequate." He was in office long enough to aid the development of the Military Academy and further professional military education in the country. Crawford's attempt to rehabilitate that institution had been impeded by controversy created by the erratic behavior of the superintendent, Captain Alden Partridge. After Partridge was replaced by Major Sylvanus Thayer in July of 1817, the academy became a source of officers educated in military leadership, and not just a training school for army engineers. Thayer reorganized the corps of cadets into tactical units, instituted the office of commandant of cadets, improved the curriculum, set standards of proficiency, and introduced better methods of instruction. Such great improvements were made in the education and military training of cadets under Thayer's 16 years of leadership that it is he who is remembered today as the Father of the Military Academy. Calhoun furthered the professional development of the officer corps by continuing the practice of sending officers abroad to study foreign military institutions. (Scott and Thayer, for example, had visited Europe in 1815 to gather military books and instruments, and to study foreign armies and military schools.) He advanced the professional experience of the officers and training of the rank and file by creating the Artillery School of Practice at Fortress Monroe. Established in 1824, the Artillery School was designed to train entire units sent there in rotation for a year's duty each.[15]

National Strategy

The allied victory at Waterloo made possible a long period of reduced tension for the exhausted states of Europe. Moreover, by 1820, fears aroused by the War of 1812 abated as Americans became aware of the more relaxed state of international affairs. Domestic challenges demanded more of America's attention. The Missouri Question and the continuing effects of the Panic of 1819 occupied the thoughts of many during 1820 and 1821. The all but unanimous re-election of James Monroe in 1820 scarcely caused comment in the nation's press. A number of debates on the size of the Army and the role of the nation's armed forces were injected into this "Era of Good Feelings" amid the continuing effects of the 1819 depression.

The discussions between the executive and legislative branches of the Government and within the Congress that led to the 1821 reduction of the Army are important, because this interchange set the tone of national strategy for the rest of the century. The public discussion was important as well, marking another step in the development of a professional army. The debate, as historian Carlton B. Smith has said, "marked a transition from the semi-amateur Army of the pre-War of 1812 era with its genuine reliance on the militia, to a professionalization of the Army, with its verbal reliance on the militia."[16]

The development of American national strategy followed a course that was different from that which had been taken by monarchs. A strong military leader, who was also head of state, theoretically could determine the strategy to be followed by his nation in consultation with none but his conscience. By virtue of the power they were born to wield, Gustavus Adolphus of Sweden and Frederick the Great of Prussia could commit their nations to a strategy or policy almost at a whim. The President of the United States, however, could set strategy and develop policy only with the concurrence of many actors, and Congress, through its control of the purse, exercised considerable influence over strategy and policy.

Like presidents before and after, James Monroe, a veteran of two wars, set forth his view of what the nation's military posture ought to be in his first inaugural address, on March 4, 1817. He described a defensive strategy that was in keeping with previous policies. But his proposals for the peacetime roles of the Army and Navy in achieving the defensive goals of the strategy were departures from the practice of previous presidents.

Monroe proposed a military policy designed to protect the nation against dangers from abroad. The United States, he warned, might become involved in a war with an enemy whose object was "to overset our Government, to break our Union, and demolish us as a nation." Distance from Europe and "the just, moderate, and pacific policy of our Government may form some security against these dangers," he acknowledged. However, the nation's vital interests included commerce, navigation, and fisheries, interests that recent experience had shown to be "exposed to invasion in the wars between other powers." These interests could then lead to wars in defense of national honor at sea or abroad.[17]

To secure the nation from these dangers, Monroe said that the "coast and inland frontiers should be fortified, our Army and Navy, regulated upon just principles as to the force of each, be kept in perfect order, and our militia be placed on the best practicable footing." Monroe's elaboration on these points was both the basis for discussion and a departure from past policy. Fortification of the frontiers was a continuation of a process already begun under President James Madison in 1816. Expansion of the Navy was also already underway. The new departure and the cause for debate was Monroe's proposal for the missions to be given to the Regular Army and the militia. Monroe expected the Army "to garrison and preserve our fortifications and to meet the first invasions of a foreign foe, and, while constituting the elements of a greater force, to preserve the science as well as all the necessary implements of war in a state to be brought into activity in the event of war . . . ." The regular forces, Army and Navy, according to Monroe's concept, ought to be fostered in peacetime so as to prepare for war; they should meet the enemy's initial onslaught and be the basis for expansion in time of war.[18]

The militia also had an important place in the President's plan of defense. The safety of the country and of everything dear to its people depended, he observed, "in an eminent degree on the militia." The principles of government and the financial circumstances of the United States would not allow the nation to maintain military and naval forces adequate to resist any invasion of its territory. The militia must, therefore, be so organized and trained in peacetime to deal with emergencies.[19]

Secretary of War Calhoun, an advocate of preparedness and a strong peacetime Army and Navy, was the ideal man to put the President's program into effect.

Occupied with the problems of postwar readjustment, the Congress did not have time during 1816–1817 to delve into an assessment of military policy. In February 1818, however, the dialogue between the legislators and the executive branch began when Chairman John Williams of the Senate Committee on Military Affairs wrote to Calhoun requesting his ideas on the reorganization of the Army. The congressional concern over the level of military expenditures, reflected in the Senator's 1818 request to the Secretary of War, grew in the shock over the depression of 1819. Fiscal retrenchment was the watchword of the Congress as it scrutinized and debated American military policy until finally taking action in 1821.

Monroe's system of defense came under its first major attack in the spring of 1820, when there was an attempt to cut the $800,000 appropriation recommended by the House Ways and Means Committee for fortifications. The movement to curtail expenses failed at the time due to general agreement on the value of fortifications. True, the program was expensive, but it could be supported as an economy measure. Much of the cost of the War of 1812 was attributed to the defenseless condition of the coast. If a single enemy attack were repelled by the fortification system in the future, the savings in lives and property would be compensation enough for the expense of constructing the system. Congress accepted this concept of economy and the fortifications program was continued, although appropriations gradually declined to the half-million-dollar level by 1824.[20]

In May of 1820, the *National Intelligencer* reported that the House had called on the Secretary of War to produce for the next session of Congress his plan for reducing the Army to 6,000 men. The motives behind this request, the newspaper reported, "were not hostile to the Army" but were in furtherance of an attempt to avoid a system of direct taxation. The alternatives were either to reduce the spending on the Army and Navy or to resort to direct taxes. The Panic of 1819 and the prevailing spirit of economy made the taxation alternative unpalatable.[21]

Calhoun sent his plan to the House on December 12, 1820. It was a good plan, but not a plan that the Congress could accept. In a period when retrenchment and economy were the avowed objects, Calhoun had produced a plan that stressed the most expensive part of the Army—the officer corps. His idea was to provide for a quickly expansible Regular Army capable of being America's mainstay in wartime. The militia, "the great national force," Calhoun said, would require the aid of regular troops if it were to be effective. "Trained artillerists and a small but well-disciplined body of infantry" were required to support the militia, who were not "capable of meeting in the open field the regular troops of Europe." The advanced state of military science dictated to him that the militia's wartime missions would properly be to "garrison our forts, and to act in the field as light troops." The peacetime Regular Army that the plan called for would be a skeletonized army of about 6,000 men, capable of rapid, staged expansion to a full wartime strength of about 19,000. It would be able "to meet the first shocks of hostilities with unyielding firmness; and to press the enemy, while our resources are yet unexhausted."[22]

Calhoun's plan to reduce the size of the Army by lessening the enlisted strength and keeping the officers of the staff and line was a significant document, even though it was rejected by Congress. The Secretary of War recognized that officers must have unique skills that require time and experience to perfect. His plan allowed study and training for the officer corps in peacetime, giving the corps a more professional footing than a constabulary reacting to the local daily problems of the frontier. Although somewhat reduced in total strength, the officer corps under Calhoun's plan would become more professional and competent.[23]

Congress received the Calhoun plan without enthusiasm. In developing its own method of cutting army strength by 40 percent, Congress helped to formulate national strategy and clarified some of the changed attitudes of the nation toward a standing army. The congressional debate revealed that the legislators agreed with the administration that the nation would only fight a defensive war for protection of sovereign rights and territory, that in a defensive war all of society would participate, that the Indians posed no threat to the Republic, and that any attack strong enough to threaten the nation would have to come from a maritime power. But the Congress did not agree with the administration on either the magnitude of the threat or the roles of the militia and Regulars.[24]

With the press and the preparedness advocates saying that it was false economy to reduce the strength of the Army, the supporters of the bill moved to show that there was little likelihood of attack. One by one, the possible enemies were catalogued and dismissed. All Europe would be too busy at home to wage war in the Western Hemisphere, observed Representative David Trimble of Kentucky. Spain could not find the means to attack the United States, since she could not even "reduce the weakest of her revolting colonies." Austria was busy controlling Naples and warding off the approach of free government. Russia could "feed ambition nearer home," and, besides, Russia and the United States found it in their mutual interest "to cultivate that good understanding which has so long subsisted between them." France was nothing to fear, and England was occupied with disaffection and discontent at home, the War of 1812 having "taught her a lesson" that the "lapse of half a century" would not "obliterate from her recollection." Representative John Floyd of Virginia looked at the world and concluded, "our peace [is] a lasting one, and there is less likelihood of collision now than there has ever been since the adoption of the Constitution. While all Europe is at peace, tired and exhausted; nay, almost the whole world reposing in a dead peace, unknown to history, I believe, from the days of Moses until the present time, with the exception of the Augustan reign . . . ."[25]

Since the major threats to the nation were seen to be in Europe, the proponents of reduction also had physical distance on their side. "Our distance from Europe," Lewis Williams, Representative from North Carolina, thought, "will always allow us one, two, or perhaps three years previous notice, and we can never be invaded without having sufficient time to prepare for the emergency." Others who supported reduction were not quite as optimistic about the length of the advance warning, but even those who foresaw only a three or four-month period of warning felt that there would be adequate time to raise and train an army.[26]

Another factor in the debate that argued in favor of a reduction in the Army was the fact that the Navy was increasing its size and capabilities. Shortly after the close of the War of 1812, the Navy began receiving one million dollars a year in funds designated for increasing its size. The Navy, naturally enough, was felt to be the first line of defense against a maritime threat. Another North Carolina Representative, Charles Fisher, went so far as to claim, "that the Navy is our proper and only efficient defence against attacks from abroad; and I, for one, will not consent to touch even a cockboat of the Navy, if, by doing so, we weaken the force of that defence." In fairness, it must be observed, that the Navy, too, was to feel the bite of retrenchment that winter—the Navy appropriation for increasing its size was reduced to $500,000 per year.[27]

The role of the Navy in national defense was clear to everyone, but the roles of the militia and the Regular Army were less obvious. It is important to note, however, that no one in Congress proposed doing away with the standing army. By 1821, even the most rabid opponents of the standing army were willing to concede that it was a "necessary evil," as Representative Williams called it.[28] Even Newton Cannon of Tennessee, a perennial foe of the Army as a whole and of West Point in particular, said that he was "willing to retain as much of this Army, in time of peace, as is necessary to take care of public arms and munitions of war."[29] The militia, however, was considered the main defense of the country in war. Even those legislators who were in support of maintaining the Army's strength at 10,000 differed with the administration and agreed with their colleagues on the militia's role. Only Alexander Smyth of Virginia, who had been the Inspector General in the War of 1812, was prepared to denigrate the militia.[30]

Most congressmen felt that the militia had a role in preserving the military science of the country. They did not like Calhoun's plan to employ extra officers in the establishment for the purpose of forming a cadre. The extra expense was only one part of their objection. Equally serious was their fear that if the Regulars were entrusted with a greater share of the defense, the militia would be neglected and the people would lose their skill at arms, thus endangering their liberty.[31]

Several congressmen felt that there was a connection between a free society and an armed populace. Though they accepted the necessity for a standing army, they urged their colleagues to remain on guard lest it become subversive. Liberty, they said, was dependent on the militia. "Liberty is gone when the military art is taught and practiced only in the standing army," warned David Trimble. If the people neglected the art of war and were persuaded to "abandon the use of arms," dire consequences could be expected: "a prostration of political virtue will ensue, that must terminate in the spasms of despotic power."[32]

Congress also differed with the administration over the roles of the militia and the Army in the early days of the war. Both sides agreed that it was impossible to maintain a peacetime regular army of sufficient size to meet wartime demands. Opponents of a reduction in the size of the Army and those who favored the administration's policy, however, argued that the role of the Regulars in the early stages of any conflict was to absorb the initial shocks of the enemy and thus buy enough time for the militia to assemble and receive training, and for the Regular Army to recruit and train a full war establishment. The militia, they said, had the potential to be the best soldiers in the world, but they lacked instruction and experience. To this group, it was "inhuman" to lead the militia into the early campaigns of war in which the decisive advantages of experience, discipline, and training all lay with the enemy. The President and his supporters in Congress saw the Army and the nation's fortifications as both the country's defense against the first onset of war and the means of "infusing discipline and power into much larger bodies of regulars and militia, which would be promptly added."[33]

The advocates of reduction, on the other hand, argued that a standing army of 50,000 men would not be adequate by itself to repel invasion. The numbers of men and amount of money required would be too great a drain on the nation. These congressmen expected the militia to provide the initial forces required to repel invasion until the regulars could be raised to full fighting strength. They admitted that by following their plan, much of the country might suffer the pollution of foreign footsteps. "But," as Gideon Tomlinson of Connecticut observed, "did any man ever expect a country to be at war and not to suffer?" New Jersey Senator Mahlon Dickerson, summarizing the position taken by the majority in both houses on this facet of strategy, had the last word on the subject: "In time of war we must have armies sufficient for the exigencies of the war; most of the fighting should be done by regular forces; but the first onset in all our wars must be sustained by our militia, and, during the war, they must be prepared at all points to defend the country . . . ."[34] The militia's numbers were expected to compensate for their lack of skill.

Congress passed the Army Reduction Bill primarily to cut government expenditures. The alternative to reduction was thought to be an increase in the national debt and direct taxes to pay that debt. The 1819 depression had left Congress wary of assessing any new taxes. By cutting expenses, the tariff would continue to provide sufficient revenue to support the essential business of government; there would be no political repercussions.[35] Moreover, Congress felt confident that the curtailment of government spending posed no threat to national security.

By 1821, a congressman could properly be convinced that the military threat to the nation was small. He could, in all honesty, see an improving Navy and a developing system of coastal fortifications. These factors, when combined with the need for economy and a basic faith in the militia—after all, they were his constituents—would allow a vote for reduction of the Army without seriously harming the country's safety. In acting as it did, Congress played its part in determining the national strategy of the age.

The national military strategy after 1821 was defensive in nature and designed to protect against a maritime threat from Europe. The means to implement this strategy were provided by a compromise between the executive and congressional plans. The Navy provided the first line of defense. In peacetime it would show the flag, protect trade, and suppress the slave trade. In wartime, it would discourage blockade and defend the ports from bombardment. To assist the Navy in protecting cities and harbors, an expensive Third System of Seacoast Defenses would be built, which would also secure the Navy's yards and bases. The militia emerged again, in theory, as a large manpower pool responsible for the initial defense in the instance of an attack, and for the provision of partially trained recruits for the wartime Army. The Regular Army, spread thin in peacetime and thus not dangerous to liberty, would police the frontier, provide a skeleton garrison for the system of forts, and prepare for war, thus providing a nucleus for a large citizen-based army in wartime.

Expansion and Internal Improvements

Between 1815 and 1860, the United States steadily and inexorably pushed its inland frontier westward. The constantly expanding frontier brought with it increasing demands for federal aid to improve the transportation and communication system in the interior. During this period, the Army was called upon to provide more than an Indian constabulary and frontier police force. Exploration, surveying, and engineering skills were also part of the soldier's contribution to his nation's development.

Exploration, of course, had been undertaken by parties of Army explorers since Jefferson sent Lewis and Clark to evaluate the vast domain he had purchased from Napoleon. *(See Map 16.)* Every few years thereafter, Army parties set out on exploratory expeditions, gradually expanding the Government's store of information about its territory. *(See Maps 21 and 22.)* As more and more territory was opened

for settlement, the nation exploited its prime source of professional engineering skill, the Army, to aid in developing its transportation network.

Problems of poor communications had long troubled the United States. Commerce, political development, and military operations were hindered by the geographical extent of the nation and the insufficient means of interior communication. Albert Gallatin's 1808 "Report on Roads and Canals" had proposed extensive federal funding of internal improvements, because essential road and canal systems were not being developed privately for economic reasons. The War of 1812 had prevented any action on Gallatin's plan, while further underscoring the need for improved internal communciations. Meanwhile, political pressure continued to build for federal aid to internal development. The War Department demonstrated its support for internal development in two important documents issued after the war. Secretary of War Calhoun's 1819 "Report on Roads and Canals" and the 1821 "Report of the Board of Engineers on the Defense of the Seacoast" by Brigadier General Simon Bernard and Lieutenant Colonel Joseph G. Totton emphasized the military benefits of a well-developed internal communications system. Calhoun expanded on Gallatin's recommendations by advocating the extensive use of Army engineers in drafting the surveys and plans required for internal improvements. He argued that good roads and canals were required for a country that depended on its widely scattered militia for defense. Such a network was the only means by which the power of the militia could be effectively mobilized at threatened points along the nation's vast frontiers. The report of the Board of Engineers (known in later years at the "Totten Board" for its 1821 junior member, the brilliant future chief of engineers) emphasized that defense required a general system that included the Navy, fortifications, interior communications by land and water, the Regular Army, and a well-organized militia. The authors asserted that inland communications were required for military supply and concentration at the point of attack, and claimed that this improvement could also benefit domestic trade and the passage of the mail; there was no reason, they concluded, that defense and commercial interests could not be complementary in a democracy.[36]

Advocates of federal aid finally passed the General Survey Act of 1824. This act authorized the President to employ both civilian engineers and Corps of Engineers officers to conduct "the necessary surveys, plans, and estimates, to be made of such Roads and Canals as he may deem of national importance, in a commercial or military point of view, or necessary for the transportation of the public mail." In practice, however, the Army, through its

West Point graduates, was the only source of the required numbers of trained civil engineers in the 1820s and 1830s. The task of surveying railroad routes was added to the extra duties of officers of the Corps of Engineers in 1826, when Congress and the President broadly interpreted the word "road" in the 1824 Act. The nation's first railroad, the Baltimore and Ohio, promptly requested and received engineering aid from the Corps. Other railroads followed suit, using Army engineers until 1838, when a change in political attitudes and an increased supply of civilian engineers, many of whom were also West Point graduates, put an end to the use of federally-paid, active-duty Army engineers for private projects.[37]

Engineers trained at the Military Academy made important contributions in scientific and technical fields other than transportation. Ordnance and metallurgy, for example, benefited from the works of Robert P. Parrott, USMA 1824, and T.J. Rodman, USMA 1841. Parrott left the Army in 1835 to work at the West Point Foundry in Cold Spring, New York. He became the head of the foundry and one of the country's leading iron workers. Continuing an interest in ordnance acquired during his Army service, he developed the Parrott rifled gun of Civil War fame. Rodman's developments in metallurgy improved the casting process for heavy guns, which allowed the production of safer large caliber (up to 20-inch) smoothbore shell guns. The Rodman guns became the principal heavy weapons of the Army and Navy during the Civil War. Parrott and Rodman's work, although cited here for its contribution to military ordnance, materially improved the understanding of metallurgy, and therefore had important civil applications as well.[38]

Civilian engineers and technicians also made important contributions to America's internal development. One of these, Samuel F.B. Morse, demonstrated in 1844 an invention that was to have an important effect on military operations in the Civil War. Morse's telegraph, which increased the speed and practicality of civilian communication, proved its military value for coordinating the movements of far-flung mass armies for the rapid exchange of intelligence information during the Civil War.[39]

Expansion and internal development inexorably forced the Army to exercise its constabulary function before leading it into a major war with Mexico. The Black Hawk War of 1832 showed the inadequacy of infantry for dealing with the highly mobile Indians of the Plains. *(See Map 22.)* Mounted troops, eliminated earlier as an economy move, were reintroduced into the force structure as a result of this brief war. The Second Seminole War, a long, grinding, guerrilla war in Florida, chewed up troops and reputations during its six-year official course. During the war, the Army

expanded to over 12,500. The reduction that came after this conflict is noteworthy chiefly because, to some extent, it was in keeping with Calhoun's 1820 proposal. No regiments were disbanded and no officers were released when the Army was reduced to a peacetime strength of 8,613.[40]

Internship for Generals: The Mexican War

Directly in the path of the surging westward thrust of the American frontier lay the sparsely settled lands of northern Mexico and Oregon. Conflict with England and Mexico over boundaries was inevitable. Americans, feeling that it was their legitimate right—their Manifest Destiny—to settle and develop the continent, were prepared to use force if peaceful negotiation failed to fulfill this self-proclaimed destiny. An impediment to boundless expansion, however, was the growing sectional conflict over the extension of slavery into new territories and states. This issue delayed the annexation of Texas for almost a decade. With "All of Oregon" demands balancing the annexation of Texas in the 1844 Presidential election, outgoing President John Tyler and the triumphant Democrats interpreted James K. Polk's victory as a mandate for the immediate annexation of Texas. Closing ranks in Congress, the Democrats gave Tyler a joint resolution for annexation, thereby obviating the troublesome requirement for a two-thirds vote in the Senate.* Mexico promptly broke diplomatic relations with the United States. After a brief pause for intrigue, Texas was admitted to the Union as a slave state in December 1845.[41]

While the trouble with Mexico over Texas continued to brew, the Oregon boundary question stirred by the "Fifty-four-forty or fight" slogan of the presidential campaign boiled to a head. Concern over English designs on California and support for an independent Texas added heat to the fires of American Anglophobia. Bellicose talk on both sides of the Atlantic, however, proved to be only talk. The British did not want to fight for "All of Oregon," and the Americans were not prepared to. They compromised, and in June 1846 the 49th parallel, the treaty line of 1818, was extended to Puget Sound, thereby settling that dispute. *(See Map 25.)*

Meanwhile, President Polk was trying to avoid war with

---

*A Texas Annexation Treaty was soundly defeated in the spring of 1844, when Secretary of State Calhoun presented the treaty in a way that made it appear as if it were a measure to extend and protect slavery.

Mexico by using the same combination of negotiation and bluster that had proven successful on the Oregon issue. Mexico, however, was not stable, wise, and worldly England. Polk and his advisors failed to understand the essential instability of Mexican politics. The only thing that all the Mexican factions seemed to agree on was that questions of independence, national pride, and honor all demanded that Mexico fight rather than acquiesce to American pressure. Polk, perhaps hoping that the logic of the American position would become apparent as the essential disparity in national power was made progressively clear to the Mexicans, pursued a diplomatic strategy of graduated pressure. The Mexicans were already only too aware of the differences Polk hoped to show. Polk did not fully appreciate either the depth of Mexican feeling or the inability of the Mexican Government to negotiate the loss of its territory. No Mexican Government could or would agree to negotiate until after the Mexican Army was a shambles, the capital city was lost, and there existed a threat of total, perhaps permanent, occupation.[42]

Polk's strategy of graduated pressure included the alteration of troop dispositions. These moves had the dual effect of escalating the pressure on Mexico and insuring that the United States would be prepared to fight should war come. Already in being was a "Corps of Observation," under the command of Brigadier General Zachary Taylor, which had been formed by the Tyler administration on the Texas-Louisiana border in the spring of 1844. *(See Map 23.)* The western boundary of Texas was one of the issues in contention between Mexico and the United States and Texas. The Mexicans, while not recognizing the independence of Texas, had insisted that the proper boundary was the Neuces River line, but they had withdrawn their troops to the Rio Grande where their effective control stopped. The Texans and Americans had maintained that the Rio Grande was the proper line, but Texas had never exercised effective sovereignty west of the Neuces. Following the annexation resolution, Taylor's "observation" force was ordered into Texas, accomplishing the move over the summer of 1845. Hoping that the boundary question would be settled by negotiation rather than force, Taylor held most of his force east of the Neuces River in order not to disturb Mexican posts east of the Rio Grande.[43]

Negotiations appeared to the Americans to be leading toward a peaceful solution until General Mariano Paredes y Arrillaga seized power in Mexico at the end of December 1845. Paredes immediately swore to uphold the integrity of Mexican territory all the way to the Sabine River. At this point an impasse had been reached, but three more months passed before this fact was realized in Washington.[44]

Hearing from his minister to Mexico City in mid-January

that the Mexicans had refused to receive him, President Polk sent orders to Taylor directing an advance to the Rio Grande as soon as possible, but also cautioning that Mexico was not to be considered an enemy unless war was declared or the Mexicans attacked. The reasons behind the order are not clear. Perhaps Polk hoped that the additional pressure would help to initiate negotiations. The Secretary of War, George Bancroft, wrote later that the President thought "that the appearance of our land and naval forces upon the borders of Mexico and the Gulf, would deter Mexico alike from declaring war or invading the United States." But if war did come, Taylor's force on the Rio Grande would be 125 miles closer to the enemy. To some, Polk's orders have appeared to direct an aggressive act. Since title to the area was in dispute, however, the President had a duty to maintain the American claim through occupation, even though later negotiations might establish a different boundary line. One must also remember that Polk and his advisors felt that they had been elected to expand the boundaries of the nation through annexation; this mission implied settling the issue of Texas' western boundary on terms favorable to the United States. Thus, Taylor's army, by now numbering around 4,000 men, or about half of the Regular Army strength, moved to the Rio Grande in March of 1846.[45]

Open fighting began on the Rio Grande frontier in late April of 1846, when the Mexican commander on that front notified Taylor that hostilities had commenced. He then crossed over to the American side of the river. At the Battle of Palo Alto (May 8) and the Battle of Resaca de la Palma (May 9), Taylor's small army of Regulars handed the numerically superior Mexicans two sharp defeats and chased them back across the Rio Grande. Taylor's elated troops were forced to halt their pursuit of the panic-stricken enemy at the river, Taylor having failed to make any provisions for crossing the river. When the pursuit was resumed on the eighteenth the enemy had fled into the interior, there to prepare to fight again.[46]

As the Americans were chasing their frightened foe back across the Rio Grande on the evening of May 9, President Polk received the first news of the April 25 Mexican attack on an American reconnaissance detachment. The day before he had met with his emissary to Mexico and heard the full report of the failure of the negotiations in Mexico City. Feeling that he was the aggrieved party, Polk was at last convinced that war was justified. The news from Taylor spurred him into action. After spending Sunday insuring that he had the required backing in the Congress and drafting a war message, the President sent his message to the legislators on May 11. Congress passed the declaration of war and authorized increasing Regular Army company strengths from the 64-man peacetime allowance to the

100-man wartime strength. It also granted authority to raise 50,000 volunteers to serve either for a year or for the duration of the war (an ambiguity that would become a problem for the army in Mexico) and $10 million to pay for the war. The President signed the declaration of war on the thirteenth and called on his fellow citizens to support the war.[47]

With the war in progress, the question of strategy at last arose. In the beginning, the administration had only two objects in view: support Taylor and seize California, objectives that of themselves might not bring a speedy end to the war. Commodore John D. Sloat, commander of the Navy's Pacific Squadron, had orders sent in June 1845 directing him to seize San Francisco and to blockade or occupy other California ports if war came. When war was declared, Secretary Bancroft directed Sloat to implement these 1845 orders and ordered the seizure of Monterrey and Mazatlan as well.[48]

Instructions for the Army were devised during the evening of May 14, when Polk, Secretary of War William L. March, and Major General Winfield Scott conferred at the White House. The strategy that emerged from this meeting looked very much like a continuation of the diplomatic strategy of gradually increasing pressure that had failed earlier. Polk and his advisors now focused on objectives that were obtainable and that if seized would apply increased military pressure on the Mexican regime. As events soon proved, however, these objectives were not decisive. The primary goal now was to seize all of Mexico that lay north of the Rio Grande and Gila rivers and west to the Pacific. *(See Map 23.)* To gain this objective, Polk and his advisors decided to send "a competent force into the Northern Provinces" of Mexico. The main force was to occupy the lower Rio Grande and what is now northern Mexico. Smaller forces were to seize Santa Fe and Chihuahua. The President hoped that this partial occupation of Mexican territory would bring about the negotiations and peace he wanted. Polk was counting on a short victorious war, followed by a negotiated settlement. He did not understand the effects of terrain and weather, time and space, or logistics and training on military operations. When Scott tried to advise him on these factors, Polk dismissed the Commanding General as being unduly "scientific and visionary in his views."[49]

The three offensive thrusts got underway and substantially achieved the desired terrain objectives by the end of 1846, in spite of logistic difficulties and amateurish generalship and soldiership. *(See Map 23.)* Colonel Stephen W. Kearny led a column of dragoons and volunteers from Fort Leavenworth to Sante Fe, annexing New Mexico by right of conquest in the process. That done, Kearny, now a Brigadier General, ordered Colonel Alexander Doniphan of the 1st

Missouri Mounted Volunteers to garrison New Mexico until Colonel Sterling Price and his regiment arrived. Doniphan was then to take his men and join Brigadier General John E. Wool's force at Chihuahua. Kearny himself set out to conquer California with a force of about 300 mule-mounted dragoons. When just out of Socorro, Kearny happened upon the famed mountain man, Kit Carson, who was carrying Commodore Robert F. Stockton's report of the Navy's seizure of California. Kearny thereupon cut his "army" back to two companies and two mountain howitzers. Sending the rest of his force back to Sante Fe, Kearny and his small force set out again for California in December, just in time to aid in putting down a revolt of the Californians.[50]

Chihuahua was the only major terrain objective not in American hands by the end of 1846. Brigadier General John E. Wool, the third ranking officer in the Army at the start of the war, set out for that objective in the fall of 1846 at the head of the center column. Wool's force was a mixed group of volunteers and a small contingent of Regulars. Volunteer units with Wool were given rigorous training and subjected to a high standard of discipline under the general's supervision. The value of this training and discipline was reflected in the generally good behavior of Wool's men in Mexico and the superb performance of his Illinois regiments later, at the Battle of Buena Vista. The advance of this column was diverted at Parras when Wool's force was added to Taylor's command. Chihuahua fell to Doniphan's hard riding volunteers on March 2, 1847. The Missourian's long march from Fort Leavenworth onward was one of the most remarkable odysseys in a war marked by long and difficult marches.[51]

The main advance into Mexico was entrusted to Taylor. Polk had reneged on his offer to give the coveted command to Scott, ostensibly because the general was too slow in taking the field. Actually, Scott was working long, hard hours trying to assemble the forces and supplies required by the Army to fight in Mexico. Secretary of War Marcy was a notoriously poor administrator, which left much of the management of the War Department, as well, to Scott. A more important reason for not giving the general field command, however, was Polk's fear that it would make Scott, a Whig, too powerful a contender for the presidency.[52]

So Polk promoted "Old Rough and Ready" Taylor, the victor of Resaca and Palo Alto, to brevet major general and gave him command of the army in Mexico. By September, Taylor had seized Monterrey after a poorly executed attack in which the gallantry of the outnumbered Americans made up for their commanding general's shortcomings. Taylor thereupon agreed to an armistice favorable to the Mexican defenders. Polk repudiated the armistice as soon as he heard of it, but the respite gave Santa Anna, the new Mexican Army commander, enough time to reorganize his forces and gain the support necessary to build up his strength to 25,000 men. *(See Map 23.)* When operations resumed in November, Taylor occupied Saltillo and Victoria and sent a force to garrison the Port of Tampico, which had been seized by the Navy. At Buena Vista, in February 1847, Taylor's forces stopped Santa Anna's one offensive of the war.[53]

American success in the north did not bring peace. In spite of the increased pressure resulting from American victories and the loss of territory, the Mexican Government would neither capitulate nor negotiate. As it became clear that the short, decisive war the Americans hoped for was not possible, Polk and his advisors were compelled to revise their strategy to force the Mexicans to seek peace. Logistical and geographical difficulties were obstacles to continued overland advance from Monterrey. The capture of Mexico's chief port, Veracruz, followed by an advance on the capital city from the east seemed to be the most promising strategy. The selection of a commander for the next campaign was as important a political problem as it was a military one. The President and his Democratic coterie were convinced that the commander of the next and surely concluding campaign would be the principal hero of the war, and thus the next President. By his inept conduct of the Monterrey Campaign, Taylor had by this time lost the confidence of Polk. Senator Thomas Hart Benton, a powerful Democrat and confidant of the President, had no military experience but was seriously considered for direct appointment to the grade of lieutenant general and command of the campaign. Finally, in spite of the President's prejudice against him, Winfield Scott was given the job. Scott's hard work and obvious professional competence had won over Secretary Marcy during the preceding months.[54]

This time Scott did not dally long in Washington. Four days after receiving his appointment to command from the President, he was on his way to the theater of war. The four days had only been enough for him to outline his requirements for the campaign, but not enough for him to insure that they would be fully met. Secretary Marcy gave the general a broad, mission-type order of the kind soldiers favor. It was also a carefully drawn document, designed to insure that the blame for any shortcomings or ensuing disasters could be shunted away from the Democratic administration and laid at Scott's feet. But this lingering Democratic distrust would not matter, because Winfield Scott was undoubtedly the best choice for this important mission. He probably understood better than anyone else, including the President, what it was that Polk wanted American troops to accomplish in Mexico, and how it could best be accomplished. Prior to his appointment to field command, the general had written two masterful papers

Major General Winfield Scott

that detailed the forces, tactics, and resources necessary to conduct an amphibious landing, capture Veracruz, and carry the fight inland. The capture of the port without a subsequent strike "at the vitals of the nation," Scott argued, would be meaningless and too costly in lives and treasure. Since Polk's terrain objectives in the north were now secure, or soon would be, the objective of Scott's campaign was to force the Mexicans to "sue for peace."

Scott knew that unchecked rape, pillage, and slaughter would not accomplish this mission. He was appalled by the lax discipline Taylor allowed in his army. Revolt and guerrilla warfare in his rear were Taylor's reward for the poor behavior of his troops toward the Mexican citizenry. In contrast, Scott would keep his forces well in hand, tolerating neither plunder nor pillage by his troops, and attempting to see that civilians were governed fairly and treated with dignity and respect. At the same time, the complete destruction of the Mexican Army was not appropriate and would in itself be too costly an objective for Scott to achieve with his limited resources. Scott had to take care not to so inflame Mexican emotions that no peace would be possible.[55]

By early March 1847, Scott had sufficiently overcome his logistical problems to have assembled a force of over 13,000 troops, including 5,741 Regulars, for his campaign. *(See Map 24.)* Just prior to the Battle of Buena Vista, many of Taylor's experienced volunteers and Regulars had been transferred to Scott's command. For four hours on the evening of March 9, 1847, the combat elements of Scott's force were shuttled ashore by the Navy in specially designed landing craft that Scott had ordered. Even though the landing was unopposed, it was a remarkable feat of arms and marked the U.S. Army's first major amphibious landing. Commodore David Conner and the U.S. Navy share the credit for this operation. The planning and preparation for the landing were meticulous; all troops and equipment were loaded in the proper order for their sequenced employment ashore in appropriate order of battle.[56]

Once ashore, Scott's men quickly invested Veracruz. The general rejected a direct assault on the city's fortifications as being too costly in lives, and instead settled down to a formal siege, featuring a sustained bombardment. The siege was a joint operation, with the Navy providing heavy gunfire support from both land and sea. Veracruz and its offshore "castle," San Juan de Ulúa, capitulated on March 29, giving Scott a base for further operations.[57]

The Americans paused at Veracruz for a few days while Scott and his quartermasters attempted to deal with the monumental logistical requirements for the move inland. Chief among their problems was a chronic shortage of transportation for the required supplies. In spite of several attempts to solve this problem, ships, wagons, and draft animals were too few for the job at hand, and were likely to remain in short supply for the duration of the campaign.

But supply and transport were only a part of the greater problem Scott faced in caring for his army. He was very much aware of the havoc that sickness could cause. He was especially concerned over the fact that the dreaded yellow fever season was about to begin in the lowlands along the coast. For that reason, Scott soon had his forces marching on Jalapa. This next objective had much to recommend it to the Americans; it was high enough and far enough inland to be beyond the yellow fever zone, there was a plentiful supply of subsistence and forage there, and the area was reputed to be friendly to Americans. Indeed, intelligence sources had reported that the Mexicans would not defend Jalapa—but the reports were wrong.[58]

Santa Anna had meanwhile seized control of the Government and was organizing the defense of Mexico City. Electing to defend well forward, he selected a strong defensive position astride the national highway at Cerro Gordo to make his first stand. Cerro Gordo was important to Santa Anna because if it could be held, Scott's men would be forced to remain in the yellow fever belt. Santa Anna also felt that his position in the rugged terrain there could not be turned.[59]

The American advance guard came upon Santa Anna's position on April 12. General Scott arrived with reinforcements on the fourteenth, increasing the American strength to about 8,500 men. He immediately ordered additional reconnaissance. The next day, one of Scott's engineers, Captain Robert E. Lee, discovered a path leading around the Mexican left flank. By noon on the eighteenth, the Americans had enveloped Santa Anna's position and routed his army of approximately 12,000 men. Scott moved into Jalapa the following morning.[60]

A division of Regulars under Brigadier General William J. Worth pushed on to Perote, occupying it on April 22. Although the road to Mexico City seemed open, Scott and the remainder of the command had to pause at Jalapa to deal with problems of discipline and manpower. Troops were being temporarily diverted from Scott to the Rio Grande to aid Taylor, and Scott also had to send back his 12-month volunteers, whose term of service was about to expire. In divesting himself of the volunteer regiments Scott also reduced the depredations committed by his troops on Mexican property. Control of the volunteers had become more difficult as their terms drew to a close. Scott remained concerned and worked hard at establishing good relations with the Mexican authorities and church officials in the areas through which his forces passed.[61]

With his reduced force, Scott pushed on to Puebla in May, occupying that city without resistance on the fifteenth after scattering a cavalry force Santa Anna had sent to oppose the American column. Taking a bold decision that Ulysses Grant would emulate in 1863 at Vicksburg, Scott then abandoned his supply route to the sea and concentrated his forces at Puebla. For three months, his troops lived off the land there while the general slowly gathered reinforcements. When Scott's numbers at last swelled to 10,000, he pushed forward again to Ayotla. This was a bold move for a force deep in enemy country with no line of communication, because it placed Scott's army within 15 miles of the capital city, thus making it subject to attack by as many as 30,000 men under Santa Anna.[62]

Santa Anna, however, preferred to remain on the defensive, taking advantage of the terrain and fortifications to strengthen the combat power of his green troops. The direct road to Mexico City was blocked by the strongly fortified hill, El Peñon. Scott sent his engineers to inspect the routes into the city. Captain Lee and Lieutenants Pierre G.T. Beauregard and George B. McClellan were among those who took part in a series of daring reconnaissances. Lee reported that El Peñon's defenses could be assaulted, but that the assault would be costly. At last, a route was found that led around the south of Lake Chalco and came out near the village of Contreras. Then, on the night of August 19, the Americans worked their way completely around the Mexican strongpoint near Contreras by marching in the rain over terrain that the Mexicans had thought was impassable. Attacking the Mexican position from front and rear, Scott's

Major General Winfield Scott in Mexico, 1847

men routed the defenders in 17 minutes, turning Santa Anna's southern defenses of the capital.[63]

Scott hurried his forces forward on an enveloping move from Contreras in an attempt to get behind the main Mexican force, which was withdrawing under pressure from another of Scott's divisions. Santa Anna gathered some of his forces into a fortified bridgehead at Churubusco to cover the withdrawal of the bulk of his forces. The fighting around that strongpoint began about noon. The Mexicans conducted a spirited defense there until mid-afternoon, when the Americans won their second battle of the day. Santa Anna lost about a third of his forces on August 20—perhaps 10,000 men. Scott's losses in killed and wounded during the day's fighting were about 12 percent of the 8,497 men engaged.[64]

Thinking that forbearance might bring peace more quickly, Scott halted his "victorious corps at the gates of the city." Consistent with his desire to limit bloodshed and leave a Mexico that would cooperate in building a lasting peace, Scott acquiesced in an armistice on August 21. Peace negotiations followed for two weeks, but they produced nothing but unreasonable Mexican demands and time for Santa Anna to strengthen his fortifications. Hard fighting resumed on September 8, and on the fourteenth the city surrendered after Santa Anna's army slipped away during the night to Guadalupe Hidalgo. With the capital occupied, a paralysis fell over the country. Small combat actions continued, but for all practical purposes the war was over. After Santa Anna resigned as head of the Government and

surrendered command of the remnants of the Army, an interim Mexican Government made peace, signing the Treaty of Guadalupe Hidalgo on February 2, 1848. In it Mexico recognized the Rio Grande as the boundary of Texas, and ceded New Mexico and Upper California to the United States; in return the American Government agreed to pay Mexico $15 million and to assume unpaid claims made by U.S. citizens against Mexico.[65]

Scott's campaign from Veracruz to Mexico City drew well deserved accolades. One of Europe's most distinguished soldiers, the Duke of Wellington, was reported to have said, "[Scott's] campaign was unsurpassed in military annals. He is the greatest living soldier." Indeed, it was a remarkable campaign. Scott had outmaneuvered and outfought an army of 30,000 troops, well entrenched and defending their own capital, without ever having more than 11,000 troops of his own. Included among those who accompanied Scott as junior officers were a number of West Point graduates—Robert E. Lee, P.G.T. Beauregard, Ulysses S. Grant, George B. McClellan, Thomas J. Jackson, and George G. Meade, among others—all of whom distinguished themselves with their leadership, daring, and expertise in Mexico. Scott recognized their contribution in his famous "fixed opinion, that but for our graduated cadets, the war between the United States and Mexico might, and probably would have lasted some four or five years, with, in its first half, more defeats than victories falling to our share . . . ." At the same time, it might be observed that while campaigning with Scott these men learned the lessons of generalship from a great soldier. The tragedy was that they would too soon practice their skills on each other.[66]

After Mexico

The Regular Army could be justly proud of its accomplishments in Mexico. It had fought well from Palo Alto to the end, and had provided a good example and steadying influence for the volunteers. The volunteers, too, had done well, as Doniphan's trek, Buena Vista, and other battles revealed. Perhaps, because of the Army's success in Mexico, no one saw a need for change in the nation's military policy. Accordingly, it remained in a static state from the Mexican War to the Civil War. One of the changes in American military policy during the war, however, was the reliance on federal volunteers rather than state militia for units to supplement the Regular Army. Although some militia units had been called forth early in the war, the Government had quickly shifted to volunteer units to fill the need for additional troops. This shift was probably due more to the nature of the war than to any revolution in policy. Because the war was being fought on foreign soil, use of the militia, essentially a local defense force called out for short periods to meet local emergencies and to "repel invasion," was not appropriate. Instead, relying on its constitutional authority to "raise and support Armies," Congress called volunteers into federal service. This wise expedient overcame at once the constitutional problem of employing the militia either outside the United States or for purposes other than to "repel invasion." The volunteers, however, were organized and commanded according to the militia laws of the various states, and retained their state identity. One important difference between the volunteers and the militia was the longer term of service. The volunteers enlisted for 12 months, which allowed time for better training. Even so, the key ingredient was leadership. Those volunteer units that had good leadership and took their training seriously did well in battle, such as the Illinois regiments that benefited from General Wool's training program, and the 1st Mississippi Rifles whose colonel, Jefferson Davis, was a West Pointer.[67]

The expansible army concept appeared to have served well during the war, and was not abandoned afterward. When the war ended, the volunteers were disbanded and the Regular Army returned to the old peacetime strength levels for its companies. There was some increase in the staff and number of artillery and mounted companies over the prewar

levels to help cover the expanded area of the nation, but the increases were nominal. Sectional crisis mounted during the years after the Mexican War, and this became another reason for keeping the Army small, lest it be used as a weapon of suppression or either side gain a military advantage from it.[68] As for its duties, the Army returned to its peacetime pursuits, acting as a constabulary on the frontier, surveying the new national boundaries, exploring the new territory, and constructing roads and forts. *(See Map 25.)*

The most important Secretary of War during the interwar years was Jefferson Davis. Under Davis' tenure in that office, some advances were made in organization, technology, tactics, and professionalism. In 1855, he convinced Congress that the Army needed more men to patrol the territory that had been added by the Mexican War. Two additional infantry regiments and two cavalry regiments were authorized, bringing the Army's strength up to 17,867 officers and men. The addition of the mounted troops made the Army better prepared to deal with the light horse of the Plains Indians. Also, in 1855, the service adopted the rifled musket as its standard arm. The minié-ball bullet that was adopted at the same time made the adoption of the muzzle-loading rifle practical, because now the rifle could be loaded and fired with nearly the same facility as the older smoothbores. The acceptance of the rifle, with its increased range and accuracy over the older muskets, required a new system of tactics. Davis accordingly sponsored the adoption of *Hardee's Rifle and Light Infantry Tactics* manual of 1855. The new system was a start, but the experience of the Civil War would be required before the effects of the rifle on the battlefield could lead to significant changes in tactics. Davis also encouraged professionalism in the Army by attempting to insure that it kept in touch with military developments abroad. He sent a military commission to Europe to observe the Crimean War and the armies of Europe. The three commissioners were all West Point-trained officers, imbued with the new, more professional outlook. The reports written by these officers on their return were important additions to the professional literature of the day. Major Richard Delafield (USMA, 1818) reported on fortifications, Major Alfred Mordecai (USMA, 1819) reported on artillery, and Captain George B. McClellan (USMA, 1846) reported on cavalry developments.[69]

Davis' attempts to resolve the problem of the command system of the Army, however, only aggravated the problem. The Secretary addressed this matter with such roughshod arrogance and lack of sensitivity for Lieutenant General Winfield Scott's feelings and position as Commanding General that a monumental public feud developed between them. It benefited no one, least of all the Army. Thus, the difficulty remained and positions hardened, making later compromises more difficult.[70] Indeed the nagging organizational problem would still exist after the Civil War when Sherman served as Commanding General. In the meantime, diverted from foreign adventures, the nation moved increasingly, almost inexorably, toward the War Between the States.

Notes

[1] *Annals of Congress*, XXVII, 232–257, 1152–1171; Maurice Matloff (ed.), *American Military History* (Washington, D.C., 1969), pp. 148–149.

[2] James E. Richardson (ed.), *A Compilation of the Messages and Papers of the Presidents, 1789–1902* (Washington, D.C., 1904), I, 53.

[3] Leonard D. White, *The Jeffersonians* (New York, 1951), p. 215.

[4] *Annals*, XXV, 1349–1351; Matloff, *Military History*, p. 150; White, *Jeffersonians*, pp. 213–215, 236–237; Arthur P. Wade, "I DEFY YOU, SIR! Bureau Chiefs and Commanders in the 19th Century United States Army," unpublished seminar paper, Kansas State University, April 1973, pp. 6–8.

[5] *American State Papers, Military Affairs*, I, 636; hereafter cited as *ASP, MA*.

[6] *Annals*, XXIX, 1851–1855; White, *Jeffersonians*, p. 238.

[7] John F. Callan, *The Military Laws of the United States* (Baltimore, 1858), p. 249; *Annals*, XXIX, 1886–1887, 1897–1898.

[8] Matloff, *Military History*, p. 151.

[9] *Ibid.*, pp. 151–154; John M. Blum, et al., *The National Experience: A History of the United States*, 4th edition (New York, 1977), pp. 175–176.

[10] Blum, *Experience*, pp. 175–176.

[11] Matloff, *Military History*, pp. 153–154; White, *Jeffersonians*, pp. 224–232; *ASP, MA*, I, 599–601, 781–782.

[12] Quotations are from a speech to the House by Representative Charles Fisher of North Carolina, January 10, 1821 in *Annals*, XXXVII, 817; Charles M. Wiltse, *John C. Calhoun, Nationalist, 1782–1828* (New York, 1944), pp. 177–179; William B. Skelton, "The Commanding General and the Problem of Command in the United States Army, 1821–1841," *Military Affairs*, XXXIV, No. 4 (December 1970), 117–122.

[13] *Ibid.*; Wade, "I DEFY YOU," pp. 10–33.

[14] Wade, "I DEFY YOU," pp. 9–10, 18–20, 33; quotation is from p. 33. Surgeon General Joseph Lovell improved the soldiers' diet and established a daily weather reporting system which eventually grew into the Weather Service.

[15] *ASP, MA*, II, 188, 190; Matloff, *Military History*, pp. 155–156; Russell F. Weigley, *History of the United States Army* (New York, 1967), pp. 144–147.

[16] Carlton B. Smith, "Congressional Attitudes Toward Military Preparedness During the Monroe Administration," *Military Affairs*, XXXX (February 1976), 22.

[17] James D. Richardson (ed.), *A Compilation of the Messages and Papers of the Presidents, 1789–1902* (Washington, D.C., 1904), II, 576–77.

[18] *Ibid.*

[19] *Ibid.*

[20] Smith, "Attitudes," p. 23.

[21] *National Intelligencer*, Vol. XXI, No. 3038, Saturday, May 13, 1820.

[22] *ASP, MA*, II, 188–189.

[23] *Ibid.*, 188–191.

[24] *Annals*, XXXIX, 755, 759–762, 766, 789–790, 826–827, 840, 876–882, 884–885, 893–895, 922–924.

[25] *Annals*, XXXIX, 881–882, 895, 923–924.

[26] *Ibid.*, 789; *The National Gazette*, February 10, 1821, p. 1.

[27] *Annals*, XXXIX, 792, 820–821; also see Rep. Wood's speech in the *City of Washington Gazette*, February 3, 1821, p. 2.

[28] *Annals*, XXXIX, 777.

[29] *Ibid.*, 826.

[30] *Ibid.*, 744–756, 762, 807–809.

[31] *Ibid.*, 776, 815–816, 840.

[32] *Ibid.*, 887–889, 776, 815–816, 840.

[33] *Ibid.*, 807–809, 759.

[34] *Ibid.*, 372, 729, 894, 922.

[35] *Ibid.*, 364–365, 367–374, 449, 715–734, 767–794, 865–866, 874–875, 892, 899, 915, 919–920, 925–926, 930; *National Intelligencer*, May 13, 1820, p. 1; January 25, 1821, p. 1; *Washington Gazette*, December 14, 1820, p. 3; December 29, 1820, p. 2; January 17, 1821, p. 2; February 23, 1821, p. 3; *Columbian Centinel*, January 24, 1821, p. 2; *Providence Patriot*, January 31, 1821, p. 3; Letter, J.J.A. to Christopher Van Deventer, Philadelphia, January 25, 1821; Letter, Crawford to Gallatin, Washington, July 24, 1819, in *The Writings of Albert Gallatin*, pp. 112–118.

[36] Forrest G. Hill, *Roads, Rails & Waterways* (Norman, Oklahoma, 1957), pp. 9–19, 38; *ASP, MA*, II, 305–310.

[37] Hill, *Roads*, pp. 40, 47, 58–59, 100–103, 128–130, 141–152; E. G. Campbell, "Railroads in National Defense, 1829–1848," *The Mississippi Valley Historical Review*, XXVII (December 1940), 362; Oliver Jensen, *The American Heritage History of Railroads in America* (New York, 1975), pp. 20, 28.

[38] Walter Millis, *Arms and Men: A Study in American Military History* (New York, 1956), pp. 93–95.

[39] *Ibid.*

[40] *Ibid.*, pp. 95–98; Weigley, *History*, pp. 159–163; Matloff, *Military History*, pp. 159–161; Russell F. Weigley, *The American Way of War* (New York, 1973), pp. 67–68.

[41] This section on the Mexican War is based on K. Jack Bauer, *The Mexican War, 1846–1848* (New York, 1974), *passim*, and Weigley, *War*, pp. 70–76 for both information and interpretation. Bauer's generous help for this section cannot be adequately footnoted or sufficiently acknowledged. Basic histories also used for a general overview were: Bernard Bailyn, *The Great Republic* (Boston, 1977), pp. 592–616 and Richard N. Current, *American History: A Survey*, 4th edition (New York, 1974), pp. 344–353.

[42] Bauer, *Mexican War*, pp. xix–xx, 1–4, 16–29.

[43] *Ibid.*, pp. 8, 11, 16–19.

[44] *Ibid.*, pp. 23–26.

[45] *Ibid.*, pp. 26–29, 33, 37; Weigley, *History*, p. 171.

[46] Bauer, *Mexican War*, pp. 46–57, 59–63, 81–82; Matloff, *Military History*, pp. 164–166.

[47] Bauer, *Mexican War*, pp. 66–70; Matloff, *Military History*, p. 166.

[48] Bauer, *Mexican War*, pp. 70, 164, 168.

[49] *Ibid.*, pp. 71, 73; Matloff, *Military History*, pp. 166–167; Daniel M. Smith, *The American Diplomatic Experience* (Boston, 1972), pp. 125–130; Weigley, *War*, pp. 71–73.

[50] Bauer, *Mexican War*, pp. 127–141, 187–194.

[51] *Ibid.*, pp. 145–159.

[52] *Ibid.*, pp. 73–74; Matloff, *Military History*, p. 167.

[53] Bauer, *Mexican War*, pp. 81–101, 201, 209–226; Vincent J. Esposito (ed.), *The West Point Atlas of American Wars* (2 Vols.;

New York, 1959), I, 13–14.

[54]Bauer, *Mexican War*, pp. 8, 23, 66, 70, 74, 86, 128, 164–166, 232–236; Weigley, *War*, p. 73; Matloff, *Military History*, pp. 168-171; Esposito, *West Point Atlas*, I, 13, 15.

[55]Bauer, *Mexican War*, pp. 83–85, 101–102, 220–223, 233–237, 301; Weigley, *War*, pp. 71–76, 489; Weigley, *History*, pp. 187–188.

[56]Matloff, *Military History*, p. 174; Bauer, *Mexican War*, pp. 234–236, 240–244; Weigley, *War*, pp. 75–76.

[57]Bauer, *Mexican War*, pp. 245–253.

[58]*Ibid.*, pp. 259–261.

[59]*Ibid.*

[60]*Ibid.*, pp. 263–268; Matloff, *Military History*, p. 165.

[61]Bauer, *Mexican War*, pp. 268–270.

[62]*Ibid.*, pp. 270–274; Esposito, *West Point Atlas*, I, 15; Lloyd Lewis, *Captain Sam Grant* (Boston, 1950), pp. 168-169, 216-217, 235-237.

[63]Esposito, *West Point Atlas*, I,15; Matloff, *Military History*, pp. 176–177; Bauer, *Mexican War*, pp. 288–295.

[64]Bauer, *Mexican War*, pp. 296–301.

[65]*Ibid.*, pp. 301, 307–308, 321, 331–332, 378–380, 384; Matloff, *Military History*, p. 179.

[66]Wellington quoted in Bauer, *Mexican War*, p. 322. See Matloff, *Military History*, p. 178 for Lee and Grant's opinion of the general. Scott's fixed opinion is found in USMA, *Bugle Notes*, 1959, p. 198, or Weigley, *History*, p. 185. On West Pointers' performance in the war see Bauer, *Mexican War*, *passim*; Weigley, *History*, pp. 183–186.

[67]Weigley, *History*, pp. 182–183, 186–187.

[68]*Ibid.*, p. 189.

[69]*Ibid.*, pp. 189–191.

[70]*Ibid.*, pp. 191–194.

Selected Bibliography

Revolution in America, 1775–1783

Alden, John R. *The American Revolution, 1775–1783*. New York, 1954. This book will long be a standard work on the Revolution. Accurate, brilliantly written, concise, yet affording broad coverage, it is a must for anyone wanting to understand the war.

Boatner, Mark M. III. *Encyclopedia of the American Revolution*. New York, 1966. As long as the reader understands that Boatner has condensed secondary sources—and is therefore liable to the errors of his selected authors—this work is a splendid source of information.

Flexner, James T. *George Washington in the American Revolution*. Boston, 1968. The second of a four-volume biography on Washington, this is an excellent study of the man during the war years. Unfortunately, the book is not always dependable in the realm of military matters.

Higginbotham, Don. *The War of American Independence: Military Attitudes, Policies, and Practice, 1763–1789*. New York, 1971. A volume of the fine Macmillan series on American wars, this book extends beyond the era of the American Revolution to encompass its causes and consequences, with emphasis on the military aspects of American society.

Higginbotham, Don (Ed.). *Reconsiderations on the Revolutionary War*. Westport, Conn., 1978. One of the Greenwood Press "Contributions in Military History," this collection of essays by contributors to a symposium held at West Point during the Bicentennial celebration provides stimulating recent interpretations of the Revolution.

Mackesy, Piers. *The War for America, 1775–1783*. Cambridge, 1964. A modern study by a British scholar. Mackesy looks at the war from the other side of the Atlantic.

Palmer, Dave R. *The River and the Rock*. New York, 1969. This book tells the story of Fortress West Point during the Revolutionary War.

Shy, John. *A People Numerous and Armed*. New York, 1976. A collection of insightful essays pertaining to key issues in the history of the Revolution. Excellent analysis of socio-political aspects and the contribution of the militia.

Ward, Christopher. *The War of the Revolution*, 2 Vols. New York, 1952. An excellent study of all the battles and not a few of the skirmishes.

U.S. Military Policy, 1783–1860

Bauer, K. Jack. *The Mexican War, 1846–1848*. New York, 1974. One of the volumes in the Macmillan series on American wars, this book is the definitive work on the war with Mexico.

Boorstin, Daniel J. *The Americans: The National Experience*. New York, 1965. A penetrating examination of American culture and values as the new nation expanded its western frontier.

Prucha, Francis P. *The Sword of the Republic*. New York, 1969. A history of the Army on the Frontier, 1783–1846, by a scholar of the American West. The Army, says the author, was the agent of empire and the instrument of order and justice on the lawless frontier. But the need for a Regular Army was thwarted by the supremacy of local interests over national interests.

Singletary, Otis A. *The Mexican War*. Chicago, 1960. A short synthesis of the Mexican War that demonstrates the close interaction of military force and political ambition; the best analysis of its kind available. Singletary puts America's first successful offensive war into the mainstream of our history.

Sprout, Harold and Margaret S. *The Rise of American Naval Power, 1783–1918*. Princeton, 1967. Excellent coverage of pertinent naval developments and operations.

Tebbel, John and Keith Jennison. *The American Indian Wars*. New York, 1960. A concise history of the American Indian Wars from colonial times until the Ghost Dance era of the 1890s. The authors focus on the cause and consequence of these racial conflicts, explaining the settlers' distrust of the Indians, the resort to force by both sides, and the development of the Government's tragic Indian policy.

Weigley, Russell F. *History of the United States Army*. New York, 1967. A useful study of the development of the Army, emphasizing its institutional and administrative aspects. Weigley's focus is on the composition of the Army and the external question of who will lead and who will serve.

Index